STUDYING FILMS

STUDYING HAMMER HORROR

Victoria Grace Walden

Victoria Grace Walden is a PhD researcher and teaching fellow at Queen Mary, University of London, and a freelance educator. She taught Media and Film Studies at A level for seven years, and has been an examiner and moderator for major examination boards. She has published with several peer-reviewed academic journals, including *Short Film Studies*, *Journal of Media Practice*, *Frames* and *Animation Studies Online*. Victoria Grace has also run workshops for Media and Film teachers in association with the British Film Institute and Media Education Association. She is the creator of the Film and Media Excellence Programme, designed to support A level teachers across the UK.

Acknowledgements

I would like to express my gratitude to the BFI National Film Archives for access to the Terence Fisher and Hammer collections, Steve Chibnall and Matthew Jones, at De Montfort University for granting me access to the Hammer archive, staff at the National Media Museum in Bradford for access to the Phil Leakey and Roy Ashton Hammer collections, and the British Board of Film Classification for access to their archival material related to the studio. I must express thanks to Lesley Walden for thoughtful proof-reading and John Atkinson at Auteur for his insightful feedback.

All production details are taken from www.imdb.com for consistency. Running times may vary from DVD copies.

First published in 2016 by
Auteur, 24 Hartwell Crescent, Leighton Buzzard LU7 1NP
www.auteur.co.uk

Designed and set by Nikki Hamlett at Cassels Design www.casselsdesign.co.uk

Printed and bound by CPI Group (UK) Ltd, Croydon, CR0 4YY

British Library Cataloguing-in-Publication Data
A catalogue record for this book is available from the British Library

ISBN: paperback 978-1-906733-32-2
ISBN: ebook 978-0-9932384-2-0

Contents

Introduction

When Enrique Carreras and Will Hinds (stage name: Will Hammer) formed the distribution company Exclusive Films in 1935, they had no plans to become horror film producers. After a wartime hiatus, in 1947 they re-established their small independent production company Hammer Films, bringing their sons James Carreras and Anthony Hinds on board. In the immediate post-war period, it was inconceivable to consider a slate of horror films. As Ian Conrich notes, 'the BBFC [then, the British Board of Film Censors] banned all "H" films in 1942, and over the next three years twenty-three films were denied certificates' (2001:98). The horrors of war had been enough for censors and audiences; there was little desire for fantastic violence on screen. In these early years Hammer adapted renowned radio plays, mostly crime dramas, for the screen, tapping into pre-established markets.

But times change. In 1951, Hammer moved into a large Gothic house in Bray, Berkshire, to save on production costs. With the introduction of the new X certificate, and the popularity of their science fiction films, *The Quatermass Xperiment* (Dir. Val Guest, 1955) (and its sequel) and *X the Unknown* (Dir. Joseph Losey, 1956) (both playing on the films' ratings with 'X' in the titles) they soon turned to Gothic literature for inspiration. Thus with *The Curse of Frankenstein* (Dir. Terence Fisher, 1957) 'Hammer horror' began to blossom as a controversial brand identity. Hammer continued to commit to horror productions until the late 1970s, when the repetitive cycle of monster films had run its course and could not compete with the new, more visceral, realist horror, emerging from several countries, particularly America. After a brief concentration on television in the 1980s with *Hammer House of Horror* (1980) and *Hammer House of Mystery and Suspense* (1984), the studio ceased production.

However, in the new millennium, Hammer has been revived. Bought by the Dutch company Endemol, the new studio established itself as far removed from the family-run business of days gone by, though it retained its focus on adaptations to some extent, with a film remake of a novel (*Let Me In* (Dir. Matt Reeves, 2010), from *Let the Right One In* (Dir. Tomas Alfredson, 2008)) and novel-to-screen translation (*The Woman in Black* (Dir. James Watkins, 2012)). The output of the resurrected studio does not have the cult following of its predecessor; however the cinematic landscape is now very different. Horror films are abundant, Hammer horror is no longer the dominant player in a niche market it once was. Nevertheless, the studio's modern films exhibit much higher production values than the classic cycle.

It is from the studio's first horror films from the late 1950s to its recent resurrection that this volume explores. The first four chapters offer critical frameworks through which to approach a study of Hammer: Chapter One introduces the production context, Chapter Two considers the British identity of the films, Chapter Three discusses genre categorisation in relation to Hammer's horror films and Chapter Four examines the usefulness of the auteur theory to an analysis of the work of Hammer's most prolific director, Terence Fisher. The second part of the book works through case studies examining how colour and the introduction of the X certificate enabled the development of a new type of Hammer film, considering the themes which are exhibited in the studio's classic films, discussing the shifts in style as Hammer began to lose financing, and audiences, and finally, reviewing changes in the contemporary Hammer films. As is to be expected in a study of this length, it is not possible to discuss every film in detail; but it is essential to discuss at least one work from the Frankenstein and Dracula cycles, and beyond this an attempt has been made to map the breadth of horror narratives Hammer has portrayed. I have specifically tried to bring lesser-studied texts to the reader's attention. None of the 'vampire sex films' have been discussed, however Auteur's publication *Beyond Hammer: British Horror Cinema since 1970* (James Rose, 2009) starts with an examination of *Vampire Lovers* (Dir. Roy Ward Baker, 1970), and the more recent *Frightmares* (Ian Cooper, 2016) includes a lengthy chapter on the more exotic examples of Hammer's output; thus it seemed unnecessary to revisit this ground when other films could be explored. Furthermore, as Hammer is most commonly examined in the context of Film Studies, this book focuses specifically on the studio's cinematic work, rather than offering a detailed analysis of the television series. This book is in no way an exhaustive exploration of Hammer's horror films, then; rather, as a guide for teachers and students (formal or otherwise), it serves as an introduction to different approaches one could adopt to a study of this particular range of the studio's work and hopes to inspire rigorous and serious study of these films.

References

Cooper, I. (2016). *Frightmares: A History of British Horror Cinema.* Leighton Buzzard: Auteur.

Cornich, I. (1998). 'X Films', in *Sight and Sound* v8 n5, pp24-26.

Rose, J. (2009). *Beyond Hammer: British Horror Cinema since 1970.* Leighton Buzzard: Auteur.

CHAPTER ONE: MAKING MOVIES AT HAMMER

Hammer's First Rise and Fall

The production history of Hammer is illustrative of the complexities of the British film industry, which has often struggled to compete with Hollywood. Though Hammer had a difficult start, it flourished into an internationally renowned horror brand. However, even the success of Hammer's horrors wore thin eventually. Its demise as a film production house in the 1970s, short-lived shift to television in the 1980s and rebirth in the 2000s expresses the turbulent nature of British film production. The history of Hammer's production practices also raises interesting questions about what constitutes a 'British film industry', for like many studios its success has relied heavily on American backing and distribution. William Hinds and Enrique Carreras established Hammer Productions and Exclusive Films Limited (a distribution company) in the 1930s. Even in the early days of production, they adopted techniques popular in Hollywood such as buying pre-existing property (particularly radio-plays) and vertical integration between Hammer and Exclusive, but the studio still ran into problems. Much has been written elsewhere about the Hammer's pre-horror history, but this chapter starts in the 1950s. By now, James Carreras (Enrique's son), his son Michael and William's son Anthony Hinds had joined the team and production had moved to a stately home known as Bray Studios which would serve as the background for many gothic horrors. By the mid-1950s however, Hammer's American partnership (on which they relied for funding) was waning, colour was intensifying competition and the rise of commercial television was affecting cinema attendance.

Hammer Horror

Hammer was able to make the transition from struggling studio to internationally recognised horror brand due to James Carreras's shrewd business sense. As David Pirie claims:

> [At this time Hammer was] out of time and out of place. All the other small self-funded British studios run by production companies were in the process of closing down or selling out to television[...] But in a way it was the very old-fashioned nature of the production set-up at Bray

which made it so ideal as a focal point for Hammer's recreation of its own horrific version of ninetieth century Europe. Bray could present the past because it was the past. (1980: 12)

Despite the many unsettling changes happening in the industry at the time, Hammer's success was, in part, due to the traditional manner in which it produced films. There was a family culture at Bray. The same crew and cast were rehired time and again, which kept productions running smoothly. Bray Studios was an adaptable space, where the rooms could be used as sets, or sound stages could be created. This kept production costs to a minimum.

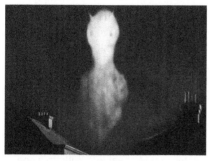

Hammer remakes television with the sci-fi The Quatermass Xperiment

Also, while other studios were, as Pirie argues, 'selling out to television' (ibid.), Hammer found a way to manipulate the new medium to its advantage. Firstly, the studio bought the rights to the successful BBC television series *The Quatermass Experiment* (1953) and adapted it into the X-rated *The Quatermass Xperiment*. Though Anthony Hinds claims the Hammer team feared television (Hearn and Barnes, 2007: 12), they came to recognise the medium as a potential source of pre-existing material, and the success of *Quatermass* would lead to a trilogy. Secondly, Hammer would show audiences what was not available on television. As Pirie posits:

> Television made the 'X' certificate important as an indicator of material viewers could not see at home. But even apart from this, it's arguable that the brashness and open audience-grabbing technique of commercial television helped spawn the kind of cultural climate in which horror films flourished. (1980: 30)

While the X-certificate enabled film studios to create more gruesome works, the same was not possible on television, which was considered family entertainment. Since World War Two, a new cinema audience had gradually emerged, one who wanted to get away from the family unit, be independent and live by its own rules – the teenager. Hammer would have to offer something that competed with television if it was going to keep teenagers interested.

While the horrific subject matter of the early Quatermass films and *The Curse of Frankenstein* were risky when the studio was so financially vulnerable, Hammer's decision to continue to reinvent popular, well-established fictions reduced the potential for failure. Even the original script for *X the Unknown* had been intended to be part of the Quatermass franchise. The studio was careful to work with the British Board of Film Censors (BBFC), though not without protest, to ensure they created content that would titillate, shock and scare the teenage market without wasting money on films that would not be granted a certificate. It was the success of their staple franchises Dracula and Frankenstein that allowed Hammer to perpetuate its horror themes well into the 1970s. The studio's decision to recycle their two popular stories parallels the serial nature of television. Thus, rather than trying to offer something completely different to home viewing, Hammer embraced the attractive assets of the medium while offering something new – X-rated horror... *in colour.*

The emergence of Hammer's target audience was shaped by cultural shifts of the time. The post-war period was characterised by financial hardship as rationing continued until 1954. However, the end of the decade saw the appearance of a more affluent society. The return of men from the battlefields in 1945 instigated a 'baby boom', followed by the gradual development of suburban housing districts to help cope with rising urban populations. As the children of the 1940s grew up, they found themselves in a unique situation. Their parents did not need them to work full-time and the Education Act 1944 meant they had to stay in school until they were fifteen. Older teenagers had more disposable income than previous generations as they settled down later than their parents, and gradually a teenage culture emerged which engaged with rock 'n' roll music, the 'angry young men' theatrical productions, and the development of sub-culture groups like the Teddy Boys (and the consequent reported rise in violent crimes and 'sexual deviancy'). As Pirie explains, this 'teenage revolution' was the first time young people had been 'identified as a distinctive group' in society (1980: 23). The teenager consumed cultural products that rebelled against the previous wave of quaint British material. Pirie, however, argues:

> Obviously horror films themselves did not reflect these social changes directly nor did they carry direct political content. However, Hammer's horror films with their visually explicit violence and thinly disguised themes of sexual frustration and release, did represent a challenge to established culture and traditions. (1980: 24)

After the success of *The Quatermass Xperiment* and *The Curse of Frankenstein*, the destiny of Hammer Productions was forever changed. The studio's colour horror films were fresh and original, and appealed to the emerging youth market. The genre became so synonymous with Hammer that even films such as *Captain Clegg* (Dir. Peter Graham Scott, 1962) (a family adventure) and the Sherlock Holmes mystery *The Hound of the Baskervilles* (Dir. Terence Fisher, 1959) were promoted as horrors.

James Carreras's intuitive business skills also helped the studio's success grow. As Pirie claims, realising their unusual position as foreign providers to the United States market, Hammer engaged in a Hollywood strategy – selling slates of films, rather than just individual ones, to American companies. Those that wanted the sequel to *The Curse of Frankenstein*, also had to agree to take the non-horrors *The Camp on Blood Island* (Dir. Val Guest, 1958) and *The Snorkel* (Dir. Guy Green, 1958) (Pirie, 1980: 14). Such an agreement increased the viability of films which might have otherwise been overlooked by distributors. Furthermore as a distribution agreement document between Quota Films Ltd., Universal Picture Company and Cadogan Films notes, Hammer was important to the American companies because the films qualified as 'British' as defined by the Cinematograph Films Act, meaning they fulfilled cinema quotas for British productions (but the American funders retained much of the profit). Other techniques the studio adopted included shooting back-to-back using the same sets, as with *Dracula, Prince of Darkness* (Dir. Terence Fisher, 1966), *Rasputin the Mad Monk* (Dir. Don Sharp, 1966), *The Reptile* (Dir. John Gilling, 1966) and *The Plague of Zombies* (Dir. John Gilling, 1966), and double-bill features. Kinsley explains that because Hammer's films were originally mostly treated as support features, the studio could get as little as twenty-five per cent of box office profits

(2008: 312); however, by releasing double-feature bills, the studio and its financiers would see all of the returns.

After the success of *The Curse of Frankenstein*, Carreras found himself in 'a position to pick his partners from the most powerful studios in the world' (Hearn and Barnes, 2007: 13). It was this combination of meticulous financial care, the personnel who characterised the close-knit production 'family' at Bray and the cultural revolution of the time that enabled Hammer to have glorious success for two decades – an unusual circumstance for an independent British studio. The film industry in Britain has always been a tempestuous business and Hammer's early history perfectly exemplifies this. What makes Hammer unusual however, is the great success it eventually mustered at a time when its own future looked so uncertain.

The Horror Rides Out

Despite Hammer's prosperity, the studio's golden age was not without its business problems. Hammer's success with the American distributors caused the downfall of its parent company, Exclusive. By the end of the 1950s, Hammer was no longer vertically integrated with Exclusive; it was now successful enough to be a standalone organisation supported by its rolling deals with Hollywood. Such deals have been popular throughout the history of British cinema and raise questions about the ability for the British industry to flourish without American support. It was perhaps inevitable with the growing global success of Hammer and its shift toward horror and fantasy themes, that the family feeling at Bray would become more fragile, and Michael Carreras, who had enjoyed the diversity of filmmaking at Hammer felt disenchanted by this new approach. In the early 1960s, both he and Anthony Hinds persisted with a more varied slate beyond the monster horrors, but neither *The Two Faces of Dr Jekyll* (Dir. Terence Fisher, 1960) (which one, of course, could argue is still very much in-keeping with the Gothic theme) nor *Never Take Sweets from a Stranger* (Dir. Cyril Frankel, 1960) did well at the box office. In 1960, Michael Carreras left the company to set up his own, Capricorn Productions, but it was never as successful as Hammer and he later found himself regularly freelancing for his father.

By the mid-1960s, however, Hammer had lost its funding deals with Columbia and Universal due to falling box office takings. James Carreras decided it was best to play it safe and focus on the products which were popular – the horror films (and thrillers, which were particularly successful with French audiences). Soon, they struck a partnership with Twentieth Century Fox, who with Seven Arts and ABPC helped finance the studio's productions between 1965 and 1968. However, Hammer's new financial security came at the cost of quality. They were quick to replace staff such as cinematographer Jack Asher because of the time he spent carefully constructing shots (Hearn and Barnes, 2007: 87). The films were now being treated like a production line, with little, if any time between projects, which put additional pressure on the cast and crew. The agreement with ABPC also had a clause stating Hammer had to play a role in keeping the distributor's studio, Elstree, in business, thus the majority of production work was moved here from 1964. The business relationships put in place to keep Hammer afloat were now dictating the way the company was run. Many of the characteristics of the horror brand that had emerged in the late 1950s – the production values, stately home studio and family atmosphere – were beginning to disappear. Hammer was a player in the global market and thus had to compromise with its many business partners if it was to be considered a sustainable investment. Their style was also affected, as Hammer developed 'a more sensationalist style of film-making [...] geared to international consumption' (ibid.), with more explicit gore and, later, nudity (elements the studio's most famous director, Terence Fisher, disliked). Hammer was particularly focused on what would sell in America because that was where the bulk of its investment came from, even to the extent of working with cult American director William Castle to produce the dark comedy horror *The Old Dark House* (1963), a film atypical of the studio's style.

However, yet again, business disagreements and a few poor box office performances caused Hammer to lose its Hollywood investors. Hearn and Barnes claim:

> Throughout 1967, Hammer's relationship with the American distributor had suffered for a combination of reasons: Fox were unhappy at Seven Arts' cut of the deal, and wanted television rights to the films for themselves; Fox were also disappointed with *The Viking Queen* and *Quatermass and the Pit*, and took a dim view when neither *The Devil*

Rides Out or *The Lost Continent* performed well in America. (2007: 88)

Once again Hammer found itself at the mercy of Hollywood, and without the support of an American distributor it would have been difficult to sustain the current level of production. A merger between Seven Arts and Warner Bros. soon saved it; however, Hollywood was restructuring and interest in funding British productions was waning. When Warner Bros'. management changed, Hammer found itself in a difficult position – the studio would only support Hammer on a film-by-film basis (Hearn and Barnes, 2007: 89). Hammer no longer had guaranteed distribution and investment, and by 1969, much of the creative personnel that had helped shape Hammer's style had left, including Anthony Hinds, supervising editor James Needs, Anthony Nelson Keys and production designer Bernard Robinson.

A new partnership with Fantale Films and American Independent Pictures (AIP) in 1969 led to only one production, *Vampire Lovers* and Hammer became desperate. The final chapter of Hammer's original horror cycle was characterised by a turn towards soft porn, influenced by Tudor Gates at Fantale (Kinsley, 2007:163), which was supposed to titillate audiences with sex, as much as violence, now censorship laws had relaxed. The studio's finance during this period came mainly from ABPC or Rank Film Distributors, but the switch to British rather than American money resulted in much lower budgets. *Horror of Frankenstein* (Dir. Jimmy Sangster, 1970) was the studio's first '100% British' film (Kinsley, 2007: 163), which, alongside *Scars of Dracula* (Dir. Roy Ward Baker, 1970), was intended 'to start the cycle again for the new generation of 70s film-goers' (ibid), thus these new films did not continue the pre-established Dracula and Frankenstein narratives.

However, competition was becoming fiercer. While in the 1950s, Hammer had offered something fresh and original, now their style was out-of-date and could not compete with the new American horrors, such as *Night of the Living Dead* (Dir. George A. Romero, 1968) and *Rosemary's Baby* (Dir. Roman Polanski, 1968). Alongside this, European and American filmmakers were producing cheap exploitation films, and there were also many non-horror films that were testing the boundaries of acceptable levels of violence, such as *The Wild Bunch* (Dir. Sam Peckinpah, 1969) and *Bonnie and Clyde* (Dir. Arthur Penn, 1967). Without the budgets Hammer had entertained in the 1950s and 1960s, it was becoming increasingly difficult for them to compete in what was becoming a saturated market of exploitation.

In 1973, Hammer began negotiations with their horror rival Tigon, but Michael Carreras wanted to retain the family business so outbid the offer. While the sentiment of his actions was charming, it was not enough to maintain Hammer's previous position in the market, although the company did enjoy some domestic success with film spin-offs from the TV series *On the Buses* (1971, 1972, 1973). In the following years, several films were developed which did not go into production, including *Vlad the Impaler*, and those that did, like *The Legend of the 7 Golden Vampires* (Dir. Roy Ward Baker, 1974) and *Shatter* (Dir. Michael Carreras, 1974) (for both of which Hammer turned to Hong Kong for support) brought problems. Michael Carreras explained at Hammer's AGM on 5 June 1974:

> Sex, kung fu and horror have maintained their hold on the 'exploitation' audiences. TV has gained further strength by showing bigger and newer 'old' films, together with an endless supply of American made for TV 'new' films. British TV companies have now started to produce films directly for TV and the UK circuits are beginning to show made-for-TV films in the cinemas. (in Hearn and Barnes, 2007: 134)

Hammer's attempt to bring kung fu into their films with the two Hong Kong ventures was not particularly successful. It was not only the lack of American backing that was harming the studio, but the growth of colour television and the shift in production it instigated. *To the Devil a Daughter* (Dir. Peter Sykes, 1976) would be the last Hammer horror for nearly thirty years and *The Lady Vanishes* (Dir. Anthony Page, 1979) would be the studio's final production of the era. Hammer stopped producing films in 1975, when much of the British industry was similarly grinding to a halt. It was no surprise that Hammer would follow trend and concentrate on television.

In 1979, two little-known Hammer executives, Brian Lawrence and Roy Skeggs were invited to continue to collect the company's royalties. In 1980s they licensed the name Hammer and produced a television series which consisted of short horror tales called *Hammer House of Horror* and later secured financing from Twentieth Century Fox to produce a series of feature-length television pieces *Hammer House of Mystery and Suspense*.

In 1985 the final episode aired but, despite attempts to resurrect the studio, no films followed.

Hammer Rises Again

Hammer's website refers to its return to feature films as 2010 with *Let Me In*; however its first production of the twenty-first century was much earlier and more unusual. In 2007, John de Mol, founder of Dutch media conglomerate Endemol, invested £25 million in Hammer Film Productions instigating the revival of the studio. This gave de Mol access to the studio's back catalogue and permission to produce films under the Hammer label. In 2008, the new Hammer Film Productions created a twenty-part web series, distributed by Pure Grass Films and published via the social media network MySpace (owned at the time by Twentieth Century Fox). While the success of MySpace was eventually overshadowed by Facebook, when Rupert Murdoch's company bought the networking site there was clearly an ambition to use it as an audio-visual distribution network. Hammer's *Beyond the Rave* (Dir. Matthias Hoene, 2008) was one of a few productions distributed this way.

Beyond the Rave *reinvents the vampire as a pill-popping immigrant*

There was much anticipation about the release of *Beyond the Rave*, with fan websites and online news articles announcing that Hammer was finally back. An exclusive premiere was held in London for fans. Online, it was distributed in weekly episodes, each approximately five minutes in length. It combines nostalgic elements referencing Hammer's past and 1990s British cinema – an era from which the studio was absent – juxtaposing Eastern European vampires, rave culture and tracksuited gangsters. *Beyond the Rave* was an attempt to cater to Hammer's dedicated fan base, while engaging a new generation. In *The Telegraph*, director Matthias Hoene says:

On the one hand there are the old fans who will always think that something new won't be as good. But we really wanted to do something fresh that would capture a young audience, so we set out to tell a story that's thrilling and sexy and a bit shocking. (in Marc Lee, 2008)

As in the studio's heyday, Hammer was marketing specifically to teenagers with the majority of advertising on MySpace. *Beyond the Rave* seemed to set a strong precedence for what was to come, however, Hammer's future slate was to be very different.

In 2010, Hammer produced *Let Me In*, a remake of the recent Swedish cinema hit *Let the Right One In* (Dir. Tomas Alfredson, 2008), followed by *Wake Wood* (Dir. David Keating, 2010), *The Resident* (Dir. Antti Jokinen, 2011) and a screen adaptation of the novel and stage play *The Woman in Black* and more recently *The Quiet Ones* (Dir. John Pogue, 2014) and *The Woman in Black 2: Angel of Death* (Dir. Tom Harper, 2014). While *The Resident*, *Wake Wood* and *The Quiet Ones* (loosely based on real events) stem from original screenplays, Hammer has also returned to its early business practice of re-making and re-purposing successful pre-existing content (though, of course, this is not unique to Hammer). Hammer is no longer the family-run British company it once was, but a part of an international media organisation under the re-established Exclusive Films. However, it has not lost its British identity, it has not forgotten its heritage. New CEO of Hammer Film Productions, Simon Oakes told *The Guardian*:

Being a British company, it's incredibly important to have a good relationship with Hollywood. Successful companies like Working Title have strong distribution links in Hollywood. Spitfire [Hammer's sister company] is an LA-based company, but the two UK principals are British. The sensibility of Spitfire is international as well as American, and if I feel that if the things they come up with fit into the Hammer DNA, then we will make it together. (in Karen McVeigh, 2007)

While it may have been disappointing for fans to discover Hammer had to be sold to a foreign organisation in order to be restored, its contemporary form is not that dissimilar to its past. Though Hammer, in its glory years, was run by a tight-knit British team, as we have seen it relied on American money and distribution – without Hollywood's support it simply would not have survived. When the American investment disappeared,

Hammer's demise was not far away. In today's global industry, perhaps more than at any time in film history, it has become increasingly complex to categorise films by their national identity. Though many of Hammer's modern films, like its earlier ones, present British locations, sentiments and characters (though it is noticeable that *The Resident* and *Let Me In* are set in America), the studio is part of a large global industry. Hammer's history teaches us that for a British studio to survive it needs to have international support and a global outlook, which is exactly the strategy Oakes seems to be adopting.

References

Hearn, M. & Barnes, A. (2007). *The Hammer Story: The Authorised History of Hammer Film*. London: Titan Books Ltd.

Kinsley, W. (2007). *Hammer Films: The Elstree Studios Years*. Sheffield: Tomahawk Press.

Kinsley, W. (2008). *Hammer Films: The Bray Studios Years*. Richmond: Reynolds & Hearn Ltd.

Lee, M. (2008). 'Hammer Horror Beyond the Rave', in *The Telegraph*. http://www.telegraph.co.uk/culture/film/starsandstories/3672065/Hammer-Horror-Beyond-the-Rave.html [accessed 15/08/2014].

McVeigh, K. (2007). 'House of Hammer rises from the dead', in *The Guardian*. http://www.theguardian.com/uk/2007/may/11/mediabusiness.filmnews [accessed 15/08/2014].

Pirie, D. (1980). *Hammer: A Cinema Case Study*. London: BFI Education.

- (2008). *A New Heritage of Horror: The English Gothic Cinema*. New York: I.B. Tauris.

CHAPTER TWO: HAMMER AND BRITISH CINEMA

British Cinema

Alan Lovell argues that the history of British cinema has been characterised by a strong dedication to realism, in its many forms (2001: 5). From the documentaries of the 1930s with a focus on social responsibility to the gritty kitchen sink dramas of the 1960s, and even the naturalistic aesthetic of television police dramas, the British moving-image industries have a strong heritage of realism. Furthermore, he claims, 'British cinema has been heavily marked by qualities like good taste, restraint [and] reticence' (2001: 8). Brain McFarlane reinforces this argument when he describes British films as being '"restrained" and "natural" and "true to life"' (2005: 1). If this is the case, Hammer horror, despite its international fame as a specifically British brand of filmmaking, does not seem characteristic of British national cinema at all. On one hand, Hammer's horrors are clearly fantastical; on the other hand, they amalgamate infrequent and abrupt moments of gore with a 'neat unpretentious realism' through the period set design of James Bernard and Fisher's controlled and methodical cinematographic choices (Murphy, 1992: 37). Furthermore, the films were lambasted in the press for not exhibiting 'good taste' or restraint. If Hammer horror challenges conventions of British national cinema, to what extent can it be understood as British?

It is significant to note, as Lovell argues:

> [That] the persistent linking of British film production with the question of national identity is odd. It has run through discussion of the British cinema for much of its history. That such a link exists is, at one level, a truism – any activity engaged in by British citizens can be seen as a way of constructing national identity. In discussions of British cinema it is taken for granted both that the link exists and that it is a politically important one – it often seems as if the cinema is the key tool for the construction of British national identity. (2001: 11)

If anything is identifiable about Britain from the films produced within the nation's borders, it is that this geographical space integrates a plurality of voices, identities and values. Lovell's acknowledgement that naturally a film may be considered British if it is created within a British context, cannot be disputed, but he perceptively claims that too much importance has been placed on the link between British identity and its cinema. One cannot simply define a specific type of Britishness from the nation's long history of filmmaking. To emphasise 'realism' as distinctly British underplays the nuances of some of the nation's most popular works, including the *Carry On* films, Ealing comedies and Hammer. Also, as Peter Hutchings (2001) argues, realism and fantasy are not necessarily binary opposites. The elements of restraint associated with British 'realism' often appear in so called fantasy films; take for example the middle-class travellers who visit Dracula's castle in *Dracula: Prince of Darkness*, whose period dress and pretentiousness towards the locals exhibits a particularly stereotypical image of Britishness. Furthermore, if, as David Pirie claims, 'the horror genre, as it has been developed in this country by Hammer and its rivals, remains the only staple cinematic myth which Britain can claim as its own' (2008: xv), then perhaps it is the studio's determination to favour excess over restraint, that ironically establishes its films as specifically British. Here, Pirie refers to the long history of the gothic in British culture, a topic which will be explored further in Chapter Three.

A very British affair turns into a deadly problem in Dracula: Prince of Darkness

Production Context

Raymond Durgnat (2011) suggests that identifying what constitutes a British film is difficult. Issues such as co-production, foreign financing, dual language and international themes complicate any attempt at such a definition (2011: 5). The British Film Institute, however, offers a useful checklist, used for assessing films' tax status, to identify whether a production should be considered British. It can be divided into four categories:

1. The setting, source material, characters and dialogue must be of UK origin.

2. 'The film demonstrates British creativity, heritage or diversity.'

3. The production and post-production work must take place in the UK.

4. The personnel involved in the film must be of UK heritage. (http://www.bfi.org.uk/film-industry/british-certification-tax-relief/cultural-test-video-games/summary-points-cultural-test-film [accessed 18/08/2014])

The test is based on a points system, with a total of thirty-five points possible, and eighteen the pass mark for a film to be considered British. While this test did not exist when Hammer films first went into production, it offers a useful framework for reflection. It is interesting to note that funding is not mentioned. Following the BFI's cultural test parameters, Hammer's films are indisputably British. Bray Studios and its surroundings provided the backdrop for the many foreign locations, which had no specific geographical space and have often been referred to as 'Hammerland' by fans. While villains such as Dracula are perceived to be foreign, they are played by English actors, such as Christopher Lee and other characters include English travellers or local aristocrats speaking with Received Pronunciation, making their origins somewhat ambiguous. Combining a mixture of Queen's English and regional accents, the dialogue of the films is unquestionably English. The majority of the tight-knit family that became the regular cast and crew at Bray were British and the films were produced, mostly, within the UK. Despite the fact much of Hammer's financial backing came from the United States, the cultural test assumes the studio is quintessentially British. It is international financial deals such as these that shape our globalised film industry today, and have done for many decades, and complicate attempts to define films by national boundaries as Chapter One highlighted.

Social Context

For audiences, one of the main identifiers of a film's relationship to national identity is its projection of specific messages and values. However, Durgnat claims:

> Like their American cousins the majority of British film-makers strenuously protest that their films have no ideological chip on their entertainment shoulder, they embody no particular message, are devoid of all preachment or indeed, personal opinion, on any important or controversial issues. (2011: 5)

Despite this contention, films as products of particular times and places inherently refer to values of that era and location. Thus, the usefulness in considering Hammer horror in relation to its British context is to understand the image of Britain it creates – with which one of the plural voices and identities does it speak and to whom? One must approach such an investigation with caution though, as David Pirie contests, it is all too easy to make assumptions about a film's relationship to the social factors of the time and place of production (1980: 19). Durgnat, however, posits that all cultural products, and indeed all matters of life, are shaped by ideology implicitly if not explicitly (2011: 5).

The success of the first Hammer horror films comes as no surprise when one considers their social context. The mid-1950s was a time of international unease, when the uncertainties of the Cold War lingered. Concurrently, in Britain, an employment and financial boom was occurring for the first time since before the war, which led to a closing of the class gap but a widening of the generational one. As the teenager emerged as a specific cultural group, it sought particular types of attractions; life was without responsibility, but full of anxiety. A slate of nostalgic, Gothic horror films which explored issues of liminality, transgression, unease and sexuality was therefore more likely to be successful from the late 1950s, than in the immediate post-war period. In the earlier half of the decade, the real horrors of war were still fresh in audience's minds. Pirie is right to be sceptical of making direct links between audience, social context and the content of films, however, as Jeffrey Richard and Anthony Aldgate argue:

> Broadly speaking, the cinema operates in two ways – to reflect and highlight popular attitudes, ideas and preoccupations, and to generate and inculcate views and opinions deemed desirable by film-makers. Film-makers select in the first case material which they know will

appeal to their audience and in the second material with which they can manipulate their audience and shape its perceptions. (1983: 1)

Once the water had been tested with Hammer's first X-rated films, the studio could mould its audience's desire by developing a set of codes and conventions that suggested specific expectations. Hammer's repetitive Dracula and Frankenstein cycles, and its progressive concentration more on Gothic horror and thrillers from *The Curse of Frankenstein* onwards evidences that while it might be presumptuous to make direct connections between social context and film content, producers (who are always looking for a good profit margin) are consciously mindful of how to attract particular target audiences at specific times.

British or English?

While close examination of the wider context of Hammer horror allows for an analysis of the films' Britishness, Steve Blandford (2007) offers a further complication to discussions of national cinema. Though specifically focusing on contemporary films, yet noting the traces of such issues in the history of British cinema, Blandford highlights not only the multitude of voices within Britain, but the plurality of distinguishable national identities. Blandford argues that there has been a lack of interest in studying or defining a 'distinctly English cinema' because 'for most people the term "British" remains synonymous with "English"' (2007: 8). However, Englishness has been critiqued as significant to Hammer's horrors. As Pirie claims, there is something 'interestingly English about Hammer' (2008: xi). Jonathan Rigby (2002) furthers this claim in his book *English Gothic*. The assumption that Hammer's gothic style is particularly English is problematic when one closely examines the films. They exhibit a Grand Guignol style (a form of grotesque French theatre) and take influence from Irish writers such as Bram Stoker (*Dracula*) and Oscar Wilde (whose *The Picture of Dorian Gray* (1891) clearly feeds into *The Man Who Could Cheat Death* (Dir. Terence Fisher, 1959)). The studio also turned to foreign myths including gorgons, voodoo and zombies.

However, one can think about the films as particularly English in relation to their messages, values and representations. Hammer's most popular narratives engage with English representations and issues: stately homes, class division, regional identity (which generally does not include Welsh, Scottish or Northern Irish voices) and superstitions. However, while many of the films display romanticised images of English stately homes and countryside, they identify these sites as places of horror and also use them to symbolise strange, faraway places (such as repeated allusions to Central Europe), despite their recognisable Englishness. Thus these films show a traditional English culture in crisis; an identity in turmoil, a place haunted by evil. This seems quite fitting for a period when a new teenage culture was emerging – a segment of society that would come to have a more dominant voice over the coming decades, and a cultural group who had a thirst for rebelling against the status quo: the way of life defined by the traditions of previous generations.

Hammer as British Cult Cinema

Though Hammer might challenge what are commonly accepted as the conventions of British national cinema, there is still something distinctly British, and perhaps specifically English about the studio's horror corpus. Hammer's original horror cycle was specifically aimed at the growing teenager market, which might encourage one to identify it as part of British cult rather than national cinema. Andrew Sarris associates 'cult' with 'an obsessive devotion to a personal canon of films which require continual and expert critical appraisal and support, sometimes in spite (or because) of their lowly, neglected or disparaged official status' (in Smith, 2001: 57). Cult cinema challenges the established norms of the medium and champions works considered vulgar, perverse and which project debased moral values: this, one could easily suggest, is the cinema of the teenager.

In his account of British cult cinema, Justin Smith (2001) identifies 1968 as a cultural turning point, when the legalisation of abortion and homosexuality, among many other major social changes, encouraged a new counter-culture cinema. While this is generally considered a period of cultural revolution across Britain, Europe and the United States, by overlooking the impetus of Hammer's horror films (which had, by this point, existed for more than a decade), and yet dedicating some detail to Witchfinder General (Dir. Michael Reeves, 1968), a film heavily influenced by the studio, Smith fails to identify the beginnings of a British cult cinema specifically targeted at teenagers, a type of filmmaking which pre-empted the counter-culture era – Hammer horror. Taking full advantage of the introduction of the X certificate in 1951, Hammer continually tested the boundaries of acceptability, and BBFC reports of their films often highlight concerns about 'decency'. In its expression of violence, gore and sexual innuendos, Hammer horror paved the way for the later wave of cult British films, such as *A Clockwork Orange* (Dir. Stanley Kubrick, 1971) and *The Devils* (Dir. Ken Russell, 1971).

Ernest Mathijs and Jamie Sexton (2011) claim that while cult cinema is difficult to define, 'cult' usually refers to an activity 'in opposition to mainstream culture', which engages a small, private group of individuals who adopt ritualistic behaviour (in a non-official, often unorganised form) (2011: 1). They consider cult films those which attract an intense following and which might be described as part of a deviant form of subculture (2011: 6). Cult films, they continue, have a 'very visible form of fandom' (2011: 7) and textually, often contain 'allusions' to other texts, and exhibit 'nostalgia', 'irony' and campness (ibid.). In this respect we might consider cult films to be texts which transgress the norms of dominant culture, while also referencing them, and films which have a limited but committed audience. Patrick Kinkade and Michael Katovich (1992) define a cult film as one that 'celebrates themes that (1) place typical people in atypical situations, (2) allow for narcissistic and empathic audience identification with subversive characters, (3) question traditional authority (4) reflect societal strains, [and] (5) offer interpretable and paradoxical resolutions to these social strains' (1992: 194). Thus identifying whether a film, or group of films, might be considered as having cult status entails an analysis of both its reception and content.

Considering both these definitions it is possible to understand the Hammer horror oeuvre as an early form of British cult cinema. Hammer certainly still has a large fan following, with magazines, online forums and merchandise available. Conventions are held and film markets advertise Hammer horror as a speciality. One might argue that the popularity of the films counters their potential to be considered cult. However, blockbusters such as the *Star Wars* (Dir. George Lucas, 1977) and *The Lord of the Rings* films (Dir. Peter Jackson, 2001-2003) have also attracted cult status despite box office takings in the hundreds of millions of dollars. While appealing to the new teenager market, who suddenly found themselves to be the social strata with the most disposable income and thus became the primary target market for film studios, Hammer horrors were nonetheless heavily criticised in the public press and marginalised by their X rating. Therefore, their audience was certainly, as Mathijs and Sexton suggest of cult films, minimal. This minimal audience composed the largest percentage of cinema-goers, but cinema attendance in the late 1950s was in rapid decline.

In relation to content, many of Hammer's horror films express the themes outlined by Kinkade and Katovich. The conflict between the naive middle-class English travellers and the Count in *Dracula: Prince of Darkness* is an example of the expression of 'typical people in atypical situations'. The beauty of the Count's abode with its picturesque appearance is reminiscent of the English countryside. Yet, there is something dark and sinister, first highlighted in the soundtrack and the quick exit of the coachman. While the travellers are represented as stereotypically English, the adventure they are about to encounter is far from typical – it is a nightmare. However, it is often not the protagonists in the Dracula films to whom the spectator is drawn; rather it is the Count himself. His seductive power and charm are both mysterious and attractive. There is sadness to his death, and the dedicated fan is rewarded with his resurrection in future films. In *The Curse of Frankenstein*, Victor Frankenstein is not a formidable man. While on the surface, at least in the early films, he appears to be the quintessential English gentleman, the audience is forever aware of the dark secrets he hides from his loved ones – his obsessive God complex and his tempestuous affair with his servant. Baron Frankenstein is an anti-hero, and it is his impious character that attracts spectators. Thus, there is also evidence of 'narcissistic and empathic identification with subversive characters', which Kinkade and Katovich identify as characteristic of cult films.

Furthermore, many Hammer horrors 'question tradition authority', though rarely in their narrative closure. The chaos and turmoil created by horrific creatures, madmen and vicious women are often resolved by the interjection of the church and white, male saviours thus seemingly fulfilling typical narrative expectations. However, Hammer horrors were renowned for their violence and sexual inferences; they were condemned and damned in press reviews (as can be seen in the examples in the case study section of this book). The conflict between romanticised English landscapes and the dark, yet alluring, horror that besieges them may be interpreted as subtly reflective of social strains at the time. However, the films, as Kinkade and Katovich suggest of cult cinema, 'offer interpretable and paradoxical resolutions to these social strains'. While the spectator engages with debauchery and gore throughout the narrative, the rather formulaic endings leave them feeling somewhat disappointed. However, when Dracula dies after Father Sandor shoots at the ice in *Dracula: Prince of Darkness*, it is the natural element which drowns him and Diana – the young, innocent woman who gives Sandor the idea. Thus while the endings, on first appearance, seem to re-emphasise traditional values, they are often ambiguous. Many of Hammer's films offer far from happy endings, even if evil is destroyed. For example, in *The Gorgon* (Dir. John Gilling, 1964), the film's young lovers are killed.

The remains of The Gorgon's *tragic love story*

Working through definitions of cult cinema emphasises the usefulness in applying the term to Hammer's horror slate. Hammer's legacy and fame has been perpetuated by a dedicated fan base, a great many of whom were not alive during the studio's heyday. Sell-out outdoor screenings of a small selection of Hammer's horror films were held at the British Museum during summer 2013 as part of the BFI's Gothic season. A large percentage of the crowd there were young adults, who were clearly excited and passionate about the studio's horror compendium. Many so-called British cult films exhibit clear reference to Hammer, from *The Rocky Horror Picture Show* (Dir. Jim Sharman, 1975) to *Witchfinder General*, and even *The Wicker Man* (Dir. Robin Hardy, 1973) in that in many respects it sets itself up as an anti-Hammer horror. Thus, to consider Hammer's horror oeuvre as the foundation of a cult British cinema would not be unfounded. It is certainly a more useful context to understand the films than the realist and restrained national cinema, most often referenced in discussions about British cinema.

Mathijs and Sexton (2011) are nonetheless cautious about the term 'cult horror', arguing that so many horror films are promoted as cult films, that the two terms are now almost synonymous (2011: 194). However, one could argue that Hammer horrors were not promoted in the modern climate when cult became a fashionable marketing device; indeed as has been argued, the term was rarely, if ever, used to describe films in the early days of the studio's horror production. Hammer horror became cult by appealing to the new teenager audience, through its repetition of alluring villains and anti-heroes (encouraging ritualistic behaviour in spectators who time and time again returned to watch the same figures on screen), and its increasing foregrounding of deviant themes and imagery. As *The Curse of Frankenstein* went into production, there was no intention for Hammer studios to be known in the future by the identity of 'Hammer horror'. While cult horror films are often labelled as such because they display bad production qualities and break taboo, Hammer's horrors may be elevated to a cult cinema beyond horror. Cult horror is a term better used to describe the exploitation movies of the 1970s and 1980s that spurred the video nasties crisis, while Hammer generally foregrounded relatively high production values for low budget films. The lasting legacy of Hammer horror and the excitement about its recent return emphasise its cult status.

Bibliography

Blanford, S. (2007). *Film, Drama and the Break-Up of Britain*. Bristol & Chicago: Intellect.

British Film Institute. 'The Cultural Test'. http://www.bfi.org.uk/film-industry/british-certification-tax-relief/cultural-test-video-games/summary-points-cultural-test-film [accessed 18/08/2014].

Durgnat, R. (2011) (2nd Edition). *A Mirror for England: British Movies from Austerity to Affluence*. Basingstoke: Palgrave Macmillian.

Hutchings, P. (2001). *Terence Fisher*. Manchester & New York: Manchester University Press.

Kinkade, P.T. & Katovich, M. A. (1992). 'Toward a Sociology of Cult Films: Reading *Rocky Horror*', in *Sociological Quarterly* v33 n2, pp191-209.

Lovell, A. (2001). *The British Cinema: The Known Cinema?* in Murphy, R. (ed.). The British Cinema Book. Basingstoke & London: Palgrave Macmillan.

Mathijs, E. & Sexton, J. (2011). *Cult Cinema*, Oxford and Chichester, UK: Wiley-Blackwell.

McFarlane, B. (ed.) (2005). *The Cinema of Britain and Ireland*. London: Wallflower Press.

Pirie, D. (1980). *Hammer: A Cinema Case Study*. London: BFI Education.

- (2008). *A New Heritage of Horror: The English Gothic Cinema*. New York: I.B. Tauris.

Rigby, J. (2002) (2nd Edition). *English Gothic: A Century of Horror Cinema*. Richmond: Reynolds & Hearn.

Richards, J. & Aldgate, A. (1983). *Best of British Cinema and Society 1930-1970*. Oxford: Blackwell Publisher Limited.

Smith, J. (2001). *British Cult Cinema*, in Murphy, R. (ed.). The British Cinema Book. Basingstoke & London: Palgrave Macmillan.

CHAPTER THREE: HAMMER HORROR AS GENRE FILM

Hammer's Type

Audiences have specific expectations of a Hammer horror film – blood, sexual references, the architecture of Bray Studios and surrounding woodlands, James Bernard's music and particular stars including Christopher Lee, Peter Cushing and Ingrid Pitt. Hammer is renowned for its horror films, despite its breadth of productions including comedies, war films, action-adventures and thrillers. Its specific brand of horror has often been considered to be a particularly English Gothic, Gothicism with its interest in the liminal, transcending traditional genre categories. It is poignant, then, that Hammer's Gothic style can be seen in some of its non-horror productions. One might question the usefulness of genre for understanding a range of the studio's films, despite the label 'Hammer horror'. Hammer brought something incredibly new to the 1950s cinema screen and it was the studio's juxtaposition of traditional fairy tale storytelling and a return to a primitive cinema of attraction interested in spectacle and experience which has arguably earned the studio such a prominent place in the history of British film.

Genre: Definition and Debate

Genre is a French word, meaning 'type' or 'kind' (Langford, 2005: vii); it has become a way to categorise films – but not without debate. Genres always have ideological, spectatorial and commercial implications. Genre serves a multitude of purposes:

> Genre as *blueprint*, as a formula that precedes, programmes and patterns industry production; genre as *structure*, as a formal framework on which individual films are founded; genre as *label*, as the name of a category central to the decisions and communications of distributors and exhibitors; genre as *contract*, as the viewing position required by each genre film of its audience. (Rick Altman, 1999: 14)

Hammer uses genre in each of these ways. The original horror 'blueprint' from which the filmmakers worked was often Gothic literary texts, such as *Frankenstein, or the Modern Prometheus* (Mary Shelley, 1818) and *Dracula* (and the *Quatermass Experiment* TV script [Nigel Kneale, 1953] before that). These fictional works were already grounded in a clear set of conventions visualised by Hammer in their own particular manner. However, once Hammer established their interpretation of these Gothic novels, they developed a rather predictable 'structure' to many of their horror films which led to the studio becoming more colloquially referred to by the 'label' 'Hammer horror'. Naturally, therefore, an informal 'contract' developed between audience and producers, and Hammer's fan base came to have particular expectations of the studio's films. However, while the formulaic nature of genres is considered fundamental to their establishment and longevity, in the case of Hammer, the repetitive plotlines, characters and themes was arguably in part responsible for diminishing audience interest in its films. Though, as Altman states, the predictability of genre films can be part of their pleasure, as spectators derive 'reaffirmation' rather than 'novelty' from them (1999: 25), *too much* repetitiveness can lead to disappointing box office figures. Predictability and conventionality are fundamental and yet troubling for genre films, which raises questions about the usefulness of such categorisation. One might argue that Hammer's ultimate narrow genre focus was responsible for the studio's demise in the 1970s, however it was also the reason for its preceding great success. It is noteworthy that on re-establishing the brand in the 2000s, executives focused on a slate of horror films, clearly understanding the synonymy of the brand with the genre.

Thomas Sobchack argues that because genres often overlap and invite categories within categories, that it might be more useful to consider 'the Fictional Genre Film as a single category which includes all that is commonly held to be a genre film, i.e. the Western, the Horror film, the Musical, the Science Fiction film...' (1977: 39). This statement problematises the status of Hammer horror – a brand which has relied on its relevance to a specific genre for decades. However, Sobchack's comment destablises our assumptions about genre categories and encourages re-evaluation of what we define as a 'genre'. Defining all of Hammer's films (horror or otherwise) as part of the same genre would encourage scholarship to reflect on patterns and themes across the studio's slate, rather than the rest of their films being mostly ignored in favour of the dominant horror texts. The developing field of media archaeology encourages such non-traditional explorations into film history – approaches which avoid concentrating on teleology, such as the evolution of a genre (Thomas Elsaesser, 1994). Thinking about Hammer's mid-1950s to 1970s films in this way would allow readings that, for example, understand the literary roots of the studio's horrors not as a simple evolution of the British gothic genre from text to screen, but as a business practice heavily embedded in Hammer's philosophy – as discussed in Chapter One, the studio regularly adapted pre-existing material for the screen. Also, such a non-linear approach encourages one to review the gothic tendencies across the entire Hammer oeuvre, for example the paedophile villain in *Never Take Sweets from a Stranger* who moves like Frankenstein's monster, and the comedy *Ugly Duckling* (Dir. Lance Comfort, 1959), which plays on the Jekyll and Hyde story, as well as Hammer's amalgamation of the Gothic melodrama and horror in thrillers such as *Scream of Fear* (Dir. Seth Holt, 1961) and *Fear In the Night* (Dir. Jimmy Sangster, 1972).

Gothic aesthetics haunt the bedroom in
Scream of Fear

Sobchack's rethinking of genre also encourages reflection on how we categorise films – does the type of film have to refer to horror, science fiction etc., or could it refer to colour and black-and-white, or age ratings? This latter idea is explored in some detail by Altman who notes the success of 'X-rated' as a marketing ploy (1999: 110) and muses on the possibility for age ratings to be a way of categorising film. While Altman specifically focuses on the idea of pornography as X (or, indeed, 'XXX') films, this idea is particularly significant to Hammer for it was the introduction of the X certificate that originally enabled the studio to move into science fiction and horror production. The X gave their films a certain status, particularly attractive to the teen market, and established expectations that these films would offer something audiences had never seen before. The introduction of colour also distinguished Hammer's work from other horror films. Genre is paradoxical, then, in that it offers one framework for categorising films, while ignoring other possibilities. However, while one must accept the complexity and problems of genre, one cannot escape its significance to Hammer's films from the mid-1950s.

Hammer is a brand which has come to rely on its relationship to a specific genre. Despite the wide variety of films Hammer produced, it is the studio's horror pictures that are most remembered. While Andrew Tudor grapples with the 'empirical dilemma' of genre (the problem of defining categorises), he asserts that one might resolve this by identifying genres as those supported by collective consensus (1977: 19). The colloquial tag 'Hammer Horror' certainly emphasises a consensus about the genre of the studio's most popular works. In light of the questions raised about genre though, an attempt to define Hammer's later films as simply horrors becomes difficult. Horror is after all a rather broad genre, with sub-genres, hybrids, parodies and international differences based on what might be considered horrific in any given time and space. Horror films can merge with science fiction, such as in the case of monster films, like *The Curse of Frankenstein*, be period pieces like the majority of Hammer's work, or thrillers with supernatural elements, such as *The Woman in Black*. So even Hammer's oeuvre diversifies. However, the Gothic is a mood which characterises many of the studio's films.

Hammer Gothic

The Gothic is an exemplary problematisation of genre. Hammer's films feature a wide range of character types, stories and iconography. However, what unites many of its works after the mid-1950s is their thematic approach and atmosphere. The traditional period horrors (such as *Dracula*, *The Curse of Frankenstein* and *The Gorgon*), supernatural thrillers and even action-adventure films (*Captain Clegg* and *The Stranglers of Bombay* [Dir. Terence Fisher, 1959] in particular) foreground notions of liminality fundamental to the Gothic mood. Gothic is foremost concerned with the liminal – the sublime, the uncanny and the abject – a world without order, beyond order and yet one in which order is restored, a world where the fears of the past and the possibilities of the future collide. The spectator is asked to relate to Hammer's monstrous creatures and people rather than its heroes. As David Punter and Glennis Byron (2004) argue:

Etymologically speaking, the monster is something to be shown, something that serves to demonstrate (Latin, *monstrare*: to demonstrate) and to warn (Latin, monere: to warn). [...] Through difference, whether in appearance or behaviour, monsters function to define and construct the politics of the 'normal'. Located at the margins of culture, they police the boundaries of the human pointing to those lines that must not be crossed. (2004: 263)

The monster's difference from us, then, points not to alterity but to subjectivity – it act as a mirror through which we can project our own repressed fears and desires. The monster is at once fearful and irresistible, we feel a lure towards them as much as we recoil away. It is the sublime, abject and the uncanny which inform monster films' aesthetics and beg the question, 'Is Gothic a genre or mood?'

The problem of definition which plagues genre theory is apparent in writing about the gothic. Punter and Byron (2004), Frank Botting (2001) and Clive Boom (2007) all agree that 'Gothic' is a term applied to a disparate range of texts, from horror and science fiction to melodrama. However, strong motifs persist across these different categories which have existed since its literary origins in the 1700s. Echoing Thomas Sobchack's (1977) idea of the one 'Fiction Genre Film', Boom posits that the Gothic is not completely definable from other forms, but rather lies on a continuum (he speaks specifically about novels, but his ideas can just as easily be applied to Gothic cinema):

> The continuum that links the gothic to the 'domestic novel' is marked by the fact that however arcane or historic, the gothic setting is always linked to the *desire* of the contemporary reader. At once escapist and conformist, the gothic speaks to the dark side of the domestic fear: erotic, violent, perverse, bizarre and obsessively connected with contemporary fears. (2007: 2)

Such a continuum can be identified through many film genres, from the romantic-comedy to the melodrama through the Gothic melodrama to the Gothic horror. Each somewhat focused on issues of domesticity, but with growing sensations of unease, and a gradual shift from the safety of the known desire to the lure of the unknown. Hammer's oeuvre is exemplary of this, from the black domestic comedy *The Anniversary* (Dir. Roy Ward Baker, 1968) through its Gothic thrillers which often focus on family issues to the period horrors, such as *Twins of Evil* (Dir. John Hough, 1971).

Jerrold E. Hogle (2002) claims that there is no pre-existing Gothic film genre and proceeds to invent it, by identifying the visual codes that define gothic in cinema. However, as Tudor (1977) warns this brings us to the empiricist dilemma, when a film is only identified as generic after it has been produced. Genre thus becomes an afterthought. Gothic as a genre or mood has been recognised and accepted by audiences for decades (if not centuries going back to its literary roots), the Gothic exists through collective consensus because audiences can identify it. The gothic then, like genre, is a very complex term. Like German Expressionism, a stylistic atmosphere which transcended genres, expressed in crime, horrors and other films, Gothic may arguably be a mood rather than a genre. However, for the sake of understanding 'genre' purely as a form of categorisation (a definition mood could just as well serve), it will be referred to as the Gothic genre henceforth.

Hammer's Gothic

Pirie believes the Gothic is a particularly British tradition. Hammer has certainly become synonymous with a certain type of British Gothic as Pirie suggests; however the genre predates the studio's creation, and even cinema. *Photographing a Ghost* (Dir. George Albert Smith, 1887) is generally considered to be the first British horror film. However, the essences of the British Gothic that haunt Hammer's films have a much older heritage. Rigby notes, that while ghosts and witches existed in the work of Shakespeare and his contemporaries (2002: 13), there was a great Gothic renaissance in the Victorian era – a macabre nostalgia for a time before science and reason attempted to explain everything, for a time when superstition was rife. However as explained in Chapter Two, the specifically English or British Gothic that Rigby and Pirie claim is illustrated in Hammer's films is problematic, particularly considering the studio's international influences.

The Gothic's transcendental quality is evidenced by its manifestation in Hammer's early, non-horror films. For example, Rigby claims *The Man in Black* (Dir. Francis Searle, 1949) – the first Hammer film to be shot at Oakley Court – includes a number of later Hammer tropes including, 'a damsel in distress, a prominently displayed coffin, a chase through the woods, an exhumation in a crypt, a moodily lit séance and a climatic return from the dead' (2002: 45-46). Hammer's first X certificate films, which are generally referred to as science fictions, also exhibit gothic tendencies. Rigby goes so far as to describe the Quatermass series (even in its original BBC script format) as 'the most gothic kind of science fiction imaginable' (2002: 49). Rigby charges Hammer's special effects artist Phil Leakey and actor Richard Wordsworth as 'discover[ing] "body horror" long before David Cronenberg' (2002: 50). He argues that there is a wide range of Gothic motifs in Hammer's early X films, including religious ambiguity, deserted landscapes at nightfall, skulls, and bodily transformations (2002: 50-52). Despite the futuristic themes of Hammer's first three X films, *The Quatermass Xperiment*, *X–the Unknown* and *Quatermass II* (Dir. Val Guest, 1957), a distinctive Gothic style was emerging.

Originally, Gothic was a term with specific historical and geographical placement, referring to the Gothic tribes of Europe known for their barbarism in contrast to the 'civilised' world of the Roman Empire. However, Punter and Byron suggest that from the mid-1700s, Gothic came to symbolise a wild, historical time which was contrasted against the restrictive modern world (2004: 7). The Gothic reflected the pre-enlightened world, the anarchic. However, they clarify that this was not to dismiss it as negative and primitive. In fact, the Gothic 'became invested with positive value in and for itself and came to be seen as representing virtues and qualities that the "modern" world needed' (ibid.). Punter and Byron's definition highlights both the Gothic's fearfulness and allure. The archaic, uncivilised ways of the past may instigate a fear of the chaotic and dangerous, yet there is something about the breakdown of the system – a rebellion and the unknown, and a Freudian desire to return to our origins that enthrals spectators about the Gothic even today. This is the fundamental uncanniness embedded in the genre, it enables us to escape the orderliness of our lives into a fantastical realm where we are free to explore but also fearful of fantasy and imagination.

Rigby argues the major iconography which was developed in Gothic novels and prevailed on screen in Hammer films included, 'dark crypts, rugged landscapes and forbidding castles populated by persecuted heroines, satanic villains, madmen, fatal women, vampires, doppelgängers and werewolves' (2002: 13). There are a wide range of conventions associated even with the Gothic. Locations may include castles, dungeons, isolated villages or deserted terrain; iconography includes crosses, bibles, candles and imposing shadows. Though Hammer's films include a variety of these, they are particularly united in their recurrent themes: isolation, repression, uncanny, transgression, transformation, suspicion, ritual and the sacrosanct – ideas which interrogate the liminal: the changing of states and the being between one and another. These notions return us to the three major Gothic themes: the sublime, uncanny and abject.

The Sublime

Edmund Burke defines the sublime as follows:

> Whatever is fitted in any sort to excite the ideas of pain and danger, that is to say whatever is in any sort terrible, or is conversant about terrible objects, or operates in a manner analogous to terror, is a source of the *sublime*; that is, it is productive of the strongest emotion which the mind is capable of feeling. I say the strongest emotion, because I am satisfied the ideas of pain are much more powerful than those which enter on the part of pleasure. (1990: 36; emphasis in original)

The sublime is thus terrifying, but grand. It is an extreme feeling, which may also, like the abject, be characterised by excess as the world around the subject resonates through their body. There can be a beauty, or an enchantment in the sublime which gives delight, if the terror is modified (ibid.). David Huckvale (2010) notes Burke's categories of the sublime which are expressed in Hammer's films: terror, obscurity, power, vastness, magnitude in building, sound and loudness and, pain and fear (2010: 80) and parallels Burke's thinking on the sublime with Peter Cushing's description of the Hammer films:

> Those older classics hold for them the delights of a joy-ride in the ghost train at the funfair, when boyfriends put their arms protectively around their sweethearts' shoulders, and although there may be some gasps and screams, they all know they'll come out safely into the sunshine again at the end of the journey, after a healthy 'scare', and enjoy a good giggle together. They love the unbelievable being made believable, and, above all, the fact that good always prevails over evil. (in Huckvale, 2010: 1)

Hammer's horror films' emphasis on relationships, from Frankenstein's secret affair to his more 'proper' engagement to Elizabeth, to the tragic love stories of *The Curse of the Werewolf* (Dir. Terence Fisher, 1961) and *Frankenstein Created Woman* (Dir. Terence Fisher, 1967) and the sexual lust that threads through a large number of the studio's later films illustrate an underlying message of the safety and pleasure of the experience – domesticity may be invaded but the desires related to it are still present. However, juxtaposed with the grotesque monsters and bloodied bodies, the sense of fear is heightened, if only momentarily. The cinematic experience of watching Hammer horror (which would have been the only possible viewing space for the original cycle) was an intense emotional exploration – an opportunity to push one's sensorium to its limits, by engaging with the shocking loud noises of the avant-garde soundtrack, the juxtaposition of horror and the lurid, bright Eastman colour, and the grotesque images of bodies. However, there is pleasure to be had in the knowledge that these films are set in the past, thus it feels as if one is looking back at a historical, rather than imminent threat, and the re-establishment of order with the monstrous defeated in the end. Like Cushing's ghost-ride and Burke's modified terror, Hammer's subliminality lies in its juxtaposition of the domestic and the horrific or the homely and unhomely.

The Uncanny

Freud explains the uncanny as that which is 'unheimlich' (unhomely). However, he emphasises that there is little difference between the 'heimlich' and the 'unheimlich' because the latter relates to the unknown and the secret, while the former to that which we keep in our homes and thus potentially what we keep secret and unknown from those outside our private space (1919). The uncanny therefore refers to the familiar made unfamiliar, or the unfamiliar made familiar. Doppelgängers, the walking or risen dead, ancient mythical creatures, are all uncanny presences which Hammer explores. In *Dracula, Prince of Darkness*, the Count's castle serves as an exemplary symbol of the uncanny. It is anarchic and feared by the coachman and locals, yet the English tourists cannot resist its lure. Upon entering they find supper laid for them and a courteous host, Klove, who, while introducing himself with a well-mannered, humble address, looms like a shadow in the doorway. The castle is both inviting and homely, and yet fearfully unhomely – it creates a feel of unease and uncertainty in the spectator, a feeling replicated by Helen who is dismissed as a hysterical woman (a stock Gothic character). It exudes a British respectability, while being distinctly foreign. The interiors of Bray Studios lend a certain domesticity to the early Hammer horror films, despite its grandeur and historical aesthetic. This contrasts the decaying, cobwebbed castle of the Universal horror classics.

The final showdown between Gustav and the Count in Twins of Evil

In *Twins of Evil*, the village men murder women for witchcraft – an act which seems outdated and inappropriate – yet there is a much darker evil, the Count. As the plot progresses, the spectator is positioned in a liminal space – the viewer's immediate feelings are disapproval of the villagers and the established authority, yet one is enticed by the lure of the Count while also fearing him and understanding that comfort and peace can only be found back in the community. The homely/unhomely dichotomy creates a continuous feeling of unease for the spectator. Furthermore, the Hammer aesthetic emphasises the uncanny more than the earlier Universal black-and-white offerings. The studio's use of lurid Eastman colours is somewhat muted today even in restored versions of the films. However, on initial viewing it was extremely bright – orange leaves, red skies, and bright primary-coloured dresses flooded the screen. While Universal played with chiaroscuro effects, Hammer exploited its position as the first major colour horror film producer, by emphasising the bright and colourful. This foregrounds the uncanny, overloading the sensorium with confusing messages of pleasure and fear at the same time. The lurid red is aesthetically beautiful, yet simultaneously terrifying.

The Abject

If the uncanny and the sublime position spectators in a space of liminality, the abject transcends it, expelling excess at every possible opportunity. Julia Kristeva (1982) defines the abject as that which enables the subject to understand its liminality, by expelling itself from the subject. It is the elements which leave our body, our blood, faeces, bile and vomit, for example, which remind us of our vulnerability, and yet our liveliness. For while their ejection is a symbol of our change and decay, their movement evidences that we are fundamentally alive. These abject essences are not objects separate from us, but essences which help define our subjectivity. In Hammer's *Dracula* the abject is present not only in the protruding fangs which suck blood from Lucy, but also in the final lingering shot. As Van Helsing and Dracula confront each other, the Count is subjected to sunlight and disintegrates, his skeleton revealed as he turns into ash. Kristeva says of the corpse and wounds:

> A wound with blood and pus, or the sickly, acrid smell of sweat, of decay, does not *signify* death. In the presence of signified death – a flat encephalograph, for instance - I would understand, react, or accept. No, as in true theater, without makeup or masks, refuse and corpses *show me* what I permanently thrust aside in the order to live. These body fluids, this defilement, this shit are what life withstands, hardly and with difficulty, on the part of death. There, I am at the border of my condition as a living being. My body extricates itself, as being alive, from that border. (1982: 3)

The lingering stillness of this shot in *Dracula*, then, both emphasises the spectator's vitality and reminds them of their journey towards death. To see the human, or more accurate human-like vampiric, form disintegrate so easily seems unfathomable, it is now just material which could float off in a gust of wind. There is a heightened sense of material vulnerability expressed by this shot. However, its stillness – both cinematically and diegetically – stands in stark contrast to the spectator, who once the credits have rolled can breathe a sigh of relief which reminds them of their vitality.

David Huckvale (2010) remarks that the good/evil dualism of the Gothic (to which we could add the liminality between the two on which he later comments) are related to the quintessential character of life:

Life at its most basic level is indeed horrific. We are born, a horror we can't remember; we die, a horror we can't record; and in between, life throws at us a myriad of terrors; the tyranny of authority, the anxiety of sex, the melancholy of loneliness, the betrayal of trust, the pain of illness and the fear of mutilation, to mention but a few. Only the peculiarly human quality of optimism has sustained us over centuries. (2010: 1)

Thus at the heart of Gothic, in Hammer's films and beyond, is an exposure of the liminality of our existence – the thin, porous borders between pleasure and pain, good and evil, the outside and the inside, the subject and the object, the homely and the unhomely. While it is tempting to explain Hammer's specific portrayal of the gothic in relation to the feelings of liminality so inherent to adolescence – between childhood fantasy and adult responsibility – the longevity of fan interest in these horror films expresses a wider relevance, the potential vulnerability of human existence and the intense feeling of pushing the body to its sensorial limits, while still remaining in a safe environment. Hammer's horrors create high intensities of affect and it is their visceral engagement with colour, flesh and sound which have particularly helped perpetuate their universal appeal. However the Gothic is very much dependent on themes which can resonant from different character tropes, settings and plots. It might be better defined as a mood which transcends genres, as is apparent in Hammer's oeuvre with the Gothic thriller *Screams of Fear*, classic Gothic horror *Dracula* and Gothic adventure film *The Stranglers of Bombay*. When a film reaches out to the limits, it can expose the Gothic.

Beyond Genre

This chapter has noted the problems with genre as a way of categorising film and there may be other labels appropriate for Hammer's work, such as a particular 'cinema of attractions'. Tom Gunning describes early film as a 'cinema of attractions' (1994: 56), highlighting that it was primarily interested in exhibition and 'the act of showing' (ibid.). It is interesting, then, that Hammer was often criticised for showing too much. Gunning's seminal essay was written approximately ten years after Hammer's eventual demise in 1986 and specifically referred to the so-called 'primitive' age of film-making. However, many consider its relevance in the age of the contemporary blockbuster (Wanda Straven,

2006). Rarely, however, has it been related to the interim period between the primitive and now. Hammer's films could justifiably be considered a 'cinema of attractions'. Aimed at the masses like the fairground ride or the sideshow – which Gunning parallels to early cinema – they engage the audience with the horrific qualities of colour (whether revealing blood or the vivid redness of a curtain), exploit the X certificate in marketing, and foreground the visceral – body parts, spurting blood, horrific music and dramatic, careful editing – which resonate deep in the spectator's body. Shifting away from the 'gritty' realism of British documentaries, they return to the style of Grand Guignol and the phantasmagoria, fascinating spectators with what can be seen and also felt. Pirie contextualises the rise of Hammer horror within 1950s teen culture claiming that, 'all three prongs of [the 1950s] cultural transformation (horror, beat music and the widespread distribution of erotic material) marked what might be called a *new freedom of sensation*' (2008: 26; emphasis added). Pirie's notion of the 'new freedom of sensation' suggests a return to the primitive desires of early cinema audiences, cinema as spectacle and exhibition. Particularly in the United States, distributors encouraged cinemas to release Hammer films as 'experiences', suggesting first aid stations for spectators suffering shock, distributing free Rasputin beards or vampire fangs for viewers, and encouraging fans to become part of the 'Count Dracula Society' through watching a 'Horror Ritual' film before *Dracula A.D 1972* (Dir. Alan Gibson, 1972). Discussing the Hammer viewing experience, the studio's long-serving assistant director Christopher Neame claims, 'the public... could cower in fright under the seat and scream freely. It was a sort of early interactive experience' (2003: 27). Thus, Hammer's style of Gothic cinema might also be understood as a particular 'cinema of attractions' targeting a highly sensualised youth market. The films were not only about seeing, but also visceral experience. However, the films combine such spectacle with fable narratives, thus are simultaneously stories and attractions.

References

Altman, R. (1999). *Film/ Genre*. London: BFI Publishing.

Bloom, C. (2007) (2nd Edition). *Gothic Horror: A Guide for Students and Readers*. Basingstoke: Palgrave Macmillan.

Botting, F. (2001). *Essays and Studies 2001: The Gothic*. Suffolk: The English Association.

Burke, E. (1990). *A Philosophical Enquiry*. Oxford: Oxford University Press.

Elsaesser, T. (1994). 'Introduction', in *Early Cinema: Space, Frame, Narrative*. London: BFI, pp11-30.

Freud, S. (1919). *The Uncanny*. http://web.mit.edu/allanmc/www/freud1.pdf [accessed on 10/08/2014]

Gunning, T. (1994). 'The Cinema of Attractions: Early Film, its Spectator and the Avant-Garde', in Elsaesser, T. (ed.). *Early Cinema: Space, Frame, Narrative*. London: BFI, pp56-62.

Hogle, J. E. (ed.). (2002). *The Cambridge Companion to Gothic Fiction*. Cambridge: Cambridge University Press.

Huckvale, D. (2010). *Touchstones of Gothic Horror: A Film Genealogy of Eleven Motifs and Images*. Jefferson & London: McFarland & Company, Inc. Publishers.

Kristeva, Julia. (1982). *Powers of Horror: An Essay on Abjection*. New York: Columbia University Press.

Langford, B. (2005). *Film Genre: Hollywood and Beyond*. Edinburgh: Edinburgh University Press.

Neame, C. (2003). *Rungs on a Ladder: Hammer Films Seen through a Soft Gauze*. Lanham & Oxford: The Scarecrow Press, Inc.

Punter, D. and Byron, G. (2004). *The Gothic*. Oxford & Malden: Blackwell Publishing

Rigby, J. (2002) (2nd Edition). *English Gothic: A Century of Horror Cinema*. Richmond: Reynolds & Hearn.

Sobchack, T. (1977). 'Genre Film: A Classical Experience', in King, B. (ed.). *Film Genre: Theory and Criticism*, New York & London: The Scarecrow Press, Inc, pp 39-52.

Strauven, W. (ed.). (2006). *The Cinema of Attractions Reloaded*. Amsterdam: Amsterdam University Press.

Tudor, A. (1977). 'Genre', in King, B. (ed.). *Film Genre: Theory and Criticism*, New York & London: The Scarecrow Press, Inc, pp16-23.

CHAPTER 4: TERENCE FISHER THROUGH THE AUTEUR LENS

Terence Fisher, Hammer's most celebrated director once stated, 'I'm only a working director' (in Hutchings, 2001:11). Fisher directed twenty-eight Hammer films between 1952 and 1974 and vehemently refused to be considered an auteur for his work at the studio. Despite his distaste for the idea, and the disputed relevance of auteur theory, auteurism offers a useful framework for interrogating the impact of this particular director within a studio which was renowned for its collaborative family-like team.

Auteur Theory

It was once in vogue to class particular directors as auteurs – the French word for 'author'. The term has specific cultural and historical roots, emerging from the French journal *Cahiers du cinema* in the 1950s. Between 1953 and 1957, critics and film-makers including Eric Rohmer, Jacques Rivette, Claude Chabrol and Luc Moullet illustrated their favour for particular Hollywood film-makers in *Cahiers*. They celebrated individuals such as Otto Preminger, Alfred Hitchcock, Howard Hawks and Fritz Lang as auteurs for expressing their 'world view' (Comolli, 1985: 198) across their films, despite their working within the strict confines of the Hollywood studio system. *Cahiers* allowed the writer who most favoured a film-maker the opportunity to write about him. Thus the 'auteur policy' (as it is better translated from the French) allowed critics to write as cinephiles - individuals with a passion for certain films and film-makers. As Hutching (2001) argues, the same passion and desire for film that influenced *Cahiers* to adopt this style of critique might also be attributed to Fisher's success: 'Terence Fisher is one of the few British film directors who seems to have acquired a cinephile following' (2001: 29). This is particularly evidenced by the writing of Pirie (2008) and the director's international fan mail. While philosopher Walter Benjamin (1968) famously argues that cinema (and other mechanically produced arts) lack 'aura' (unlike, for example, painting, which retains the subjectivity of its artists), the *Cahiers* critics imply that some films retain an artistic aura, or signature, and in their writing they suggest that such works might be considered art in comparison with other mass cultural entertainment products that dominate the market.

Though André Bazin is often credited with establishing the concept of the auteur, his essay 'On the Politique des Auteurs' criticises the exclusive approach of the auteur policy. However he considers it a framework which enables analysis of the 'contributions of the artists [...] quite apart from the qualities of the subject of the technique: i.e. the man behinds the style' (1985:256). Bazin claims the auteur should be considered 'someone who speaks in the first person' (1985: 253), thus a film-maker whose personal voice can be heard. However, he also believes it is important to consider the 'genius of the system' (1985: 258). Bazin's peers at *Cahiers* soon followed him with concerns about the approach in a published discussion in 1965 (Cormolli, 1985), but they highlight the policy's usefulness: it elevates the status of particular American films and directors, thus refusing to tar the entire Hollywood industry with the same brush, shifts from ideological analysis to value judgment and introduces a type of film criticism which is primarily interested in aesthetics and themes. Though it is evident the *Cahiers* critics were specifically interested in particular American directors who projected their worldview despite the restrictions of the studio system, and within twenty years were concerned that the auteur policy had become a fixed framework, their work did highlight some of the most fascinating film-makers of the era.

Fisher entered the film industry in his late twenties, worked in minor roles before becoming an editor and director, and spent most of his career in B-movies, including working for Hammer regularly. He is hardly comparable to the likes of Hitchcock and Lang. As the opening statement of this chapter highlights, he certainly did not claim to project a specific 'world view'; however, considering his work from the auteur approach – a cinephilic celebration – enables a close analysis of his contributions and examines whether it is possible for a director to project their 'world view' without consciously aiming to do so. As Michel Mardore claims in the *Cahiers* dialogue:

> We no longer have the right to overlook happy accidents in the name of some absolute *politique des auteurs* because the time has come to envisage an open cinema, that is a non-dogmatic cinema. In such a perspective everyone has their chance. This does not mean throwing over theories and alliances, it means a total approach to cinema. (in Cormolli, 1985: 202)

Thus one must be cautious in using auteurism to narrowly identify the masters of the medium while ignoring the rest, but it can work alongside the other approaches applied in this book, including cultural context, industry, genre and close analysis, to enrich one's reading of a body of work. By exploring patterns across Fisher's work, it is possible to identify his contribution to Hammer's films, without elevating his involvement as more significant than that of others. As it was a cinephilic tendency that encouraged the *Cahiers* critics to muse about their favourite Hollywood directors, so a great fan base persists that celebrates Hammer, and particularly Fisher's films.

American critic Andrew Sarris's approach to auteurism attempts to grade directors by three levels, assuming only the auteur is capable of all:

1. 'The technical competence of a director.'

2. 'The distinguishable personality of the director' (revealed through the film's style).

3. 'The interior meaning, the ultimate glory of the cinema as art.' (1962: 7)

However, Pauline Kael disputes Sarris. She argues that repeated patterns in director's work are not always a sign of quality: 'it may be necessary to point out to auteur critics that repetition without development is decline' (1963: 47). In Hammer's case, while Fisher's motifs did become somewhat repetitive, the shift from his formula to that of the more explicit styles of Freddie Francis and Roy Ward Baker could be considered the beginning of the studio's decline aesthetically and eventually financially. On the other hand, Hammer had been running out of ideas by the mid-1960s, thus one could speculate that had the Fisher-Sangster-Hinds team continued to create productions like *The Curse of Frankenstein*, *Dracula* and *The Mummy* (Dir. Terence Fisher, 1959) with collaborators James Bernard, Jack Asher, James Need, Bernard Robinson and actors Peter Cushing and Christopher Lee, then perhaps the horror franchise would have declined much earlier than it did. Though the studio's later films were rarely as successful as the acknowledged classics, the studio at least attempted to broaden its horizon in horror and beyond.

Kael also contests that the auteur theory ignores the collaborative process of filmmaking (1963: 46). Producers, financiers, actors and censors can all have a significant influence over the content and style of a final production, and this was certainly true for Hammer (as discussed in Chapter One). Kael's criticisms are noteworthy and raise questions about the usefulness of the auteur theory beyond the *Cahiers* critics' original intentions. Considering her argument, one might regard an auteur approach to Terence Fisher's films as an investigation into whether the films he directed are particularly distinguishable from later Hammer horror films, thus allowing one to analyse whether the collective identity of the Hammer ensemble and its establishment as a brand overshadows personal style. One must note the wider issues at stake when considering such a collective process as influenced by only one individual at any given time. However, Peter Wollen believes an auteur approach to film analysis 'involves a kind of decipherment, decryptment' (2000: 77). He argues that delving beneath the 'noise' from the producer, camera crew and other contributors, it is possible to consider the specific 'directional factor' that has shaped a film (ibid.). Thus it is still possible to see the usefulness in approaching a close study of Fisher's work to identify whether his films are distinct from the rest of Hammer's horror oeuvre. Against a macro analysis of the studio's production history, genre and cultural identity, and a micro analysis of a series of films, a focus on the work of a particular director working for Hammer enables a more rounded understanding of the studio's horror era.

Terence Fisher

Background

In his detailed biography of Terence Fisher, Peter Hutchings (2001), while personally sceptical of the auteur theory, illuminates the importance of considering the director's role in production. Also, he thoughtfully posits that not every director has the same job description (2001: 25). Some, like Hitchcock had more autonomy over their work, while those like Fisher were part of a larger collaborative team. Hutching argues, however, that to simply place Fisher in opposition to such major film-makers is to do a disservice 'both to Fisher and to the industry that helped form him as a film director' (ibid.). Fisher's early Hammer horrors have often been described as 'pedestrian, over-literal and cinematically lifeless' (Forshaw, 2013: 59). In contrast, critics like G.R. Parfitt defend Fisher against such claims, even putting him on par with traditional 'auteur' directors: 'I will admit that I think Terry Fisher is one fantastic director – and the most important force in the fantasy film genre in the last twenty years. Fisher and John Ford stand at the top of my list' (1974: 49).

Before his work with Hammer, it would have been difficult to recognise Fisher's contribution to the British film industry as particularly significant. He was a late starter, working as a clapper boy at the age of twenty-nine after serving in the Merchant Navy. He then worked as an editor from 1936 until 1947, when he shoot his first film as director, the supernatural comedy *Colonel Bogey* (1948; his only horror and costume film before *The Curse of Frankenstein*). He worked for Highbury Studios and then Gainsborough (both owned by Rank at the time) until the latter's demise in the early 1950s. Not having any particularly acclaimed works to his name at this point, Fisher found himself working in the low-budget sector into the early 1950s on numerous B-movie shorts designed to support main features. During this time, many of the films he directed were science fictions and crime thrillers and on several occasions he found himself working with Hammer. Before *The Curse of Frankenstein*, Fisher had already directed eleven films for the studio and would continue to be their main director until the failure of *The Phantom of the Opera* (Dir. Terence Fisher, 1962), after which he would only work on six more Hammer productions over twelve years.

Fisher's move into horror was accidental. As he famously claimed, he was 'just the hack Hammer owed a picture to' (Pirie, 2008: 33). He had been hired to direct the *Black Opal*, but filming was cancelled and an agreement of future work made. Though Fisher never admits to a specific directorial style, Hammer's Anthony Hinds felt Fisher under-rated himself. It is often stated that it was Fisher's impressive earlier work with Hammer, notably the science fiction *Four-Sided Triangle* (Dir. Terence Fisher, 1953) which encouraged Hinds to ask the director to work on *The Curse of Frankenstein*. It seems Fisher's peers saw something in his work that he did not. Hinds identified a particular style in Fisher's previous work. Hutching argues that even in Fisher's early works, themes and techniques were emerging that would be prominent in the horror films he directed for Hammer. For example, his immobile camera set-ups and 'a sense of desire as a dangerously uncontrollable force' – both evident, for example in *The Astonished Heart* (Dir. Anthony Darnborough & Terence Fisher, 1950) (2001: 35-36). However, Hutchings is careful to note that any conventionality present in some of Fisher's earlier films may relate to the limitations imposed on him by production processes at Highbury, where he was working on low budget productions with tight schedules: projects used as a training ground for the young talent known as the 'Charm School' (2001: 43). While Hutchings suggests that Fisher came into his own upon directing *The Curse of Frankenstein*, his analysis of the director's work at Hammer suggests that Fisher was always learning and, like most directors, there were films amongst his oeuvre that were carefully crafted and others with which he was not satisfied, such as *The Stranglers of Bombay*. Nevertheless, while Fisher claimed to be a 'hack director', who did whatever work he was given, his notes in the National Film Archive suggest he did turn down projects which were 'outside of what I feel I do best' (Fisher, ND). He did have a favoured style.

Fisher's Style

Fisher detested the 'horror' tag applied to his films at Hammer, preferring to think of them as adult fairy tales, and he presented them appropriately in a period setting and in non-specific Central European locations, in places temporally and spatially distant from his intended audience. He appreciated the cinema as a place for escapism and entertainment. Horror for Fisher was something more relevant to the real world:

> I think horror is a very loose word. I find some of the contemporary sex, drug and violence films far more horrible than anything I have ever made. Which generally speaking deal in fantasy and superstition - they deal with contemporary life. What I mean is I try and make the unreal true and believable, at least while the audience is watching it. (in Parfitt, 1974: 52)

Fisher's films are mostly, apart from a few of the later ones in which he felt pressurised to pander to the market, much more restrained than critics give him credit for. *The Curse of Frankenstein* has hardly any blood, and while he is considered the first director to show blood spurting from a body (Harry Ringel, 1975: 10), he did so sparingly, much less than other

Hammer directors such as Freddie Francis, whose opening in *Dracula has Risen from the Grave* (Dir. Freddie Francis, 1968) is more graphic than Fisher's work. A bell ringer discovers blood on the ropes; he investigates the belfry and screams. Then the camera slowly reveals blood trails before a woman is found hanging upside-down in the bell with bite marks on her neck emphasised in close-up. While Fisher's bloody opening to *Dracula* is iconic, there is little further blood in the film; in contrast, Francis regularly threw 'Kensington Gore' (Hammer's blood mixture) across sets and exploited lurid colourisation.

Murphy notes that Francis's experience as a camera operator seems to have influenced his heavily voyeuristic style and avant-garde colourisation (1992: 175). Another Hammer director, Don Sharp's 'fluid camera and frequent dissolves' were more similar to Roger Corman's style than Fisher's (Murphy, 1992: 169), while Roy Ward Baker's films exhibit a 'crassness' of visual excess (Murphy, 1992: 176). Fisher's careful tension between a restrained, slow, period realism and abrupt, shocking moments of horror continued to influence later Hammer directors, but each director brought a distinct style to the studio. By Hammer's Karnstein trilogy and modern-day Dracula films, with which Fisher was not involved, the studio had moved away from his restrained style to a more explicit, fast-paced and soft porn approach.

Seeing himself as a fairy tale film-maker rather than horror specialist, it comes as no surprise that Fisher's influences were rather disparate; however, their effect can clearly be seen in his work. As Harry Ringel claims, Fisher appreciated the French New Wave, *Peeping Tom* (Dir. Michael Powell, 1960) and Hitchcock, acknowledging the latter 'as the world's master storyteller', but criticising his films for having no heart (1975: 5). While Hitchcock famously referred to his cast as mere props, Fisher attempted to foreground the human condition in all of his films, in both human and non-human characters. Fisher was an actor's director and greatly believed in the value of less pre-planning and thorough rehearsing, seeing how the actors moved in the space and interacted with each other (Kinsley, 1999: 94). While one could criticise this as a lack of directorial authority, modern film-makers such as Mike Leigh are celebrated for their improvisational technique, thus it would be unfair to see this as a fault in Fisher's technique. Ringel identifies another interesting influence on Fisher's work, that of the love story specialist

Frank Borzage, who Fisher believed was 'the greatest director in the world' (1975: 5). One of the charms of Fisher's films is the endearing and often tragic love story at their root. He even manages to inject some romance into Hammer's heartless version of the Frankenstein myth in *Frankenstein Created Woman*. Hans and Christian, whose love is forbidden by her father, are united in the same body. Fisher reluctantly directed a rape scene in *Frankenstein Must Be Destroyed* (Dir. Terence Fisher, 1969), a scene designed to titillate audiences, when the studio was in financial crisis (Kinsley, 2007: 111). Romance is a major theme in many of his films, including *The Phantom of the Opera*, *The Mummy* and *The Curse of the Werewolf*.

While one can quite rightly argue themes are defined by script rather than director, and tragic romance transcends Fisher's Hammer films, he clearly exerted more authority over such matters than he claims. This is nowhere more evident than in his depiction of Frankenstein. As Ringel posits, Fisher

> found a spiritual ally in Peter Cushing. Older men than their 22 year old scriptwriter [Sangster], they sensed a metaphysical incorrectness much larger than Sangster's pride-based concept: the supra-moral dilemma of a man happily overcommitted to his vision, but blind to the emotional death within him. (1975: 6)

Sangster remade the Baron's tale as *The Horror of Frankenstein* with a youthful dandy Baron. The character lost the complexity of the Fisher-Cushing creation and the film was one of Hammer's least successful. Furthermore, Sangster's *The Curse of Frankenstein* script is sparse in description; therefore there was much room for interpretation and, as Paul M. Jensen argues, much of Sangster's script was either re-written or dialogue replaced with visuals by Fisher (1996: 159). Fisher clearly exerted more creative influence than for which he took credit and was a humble director who respected the great talent that surrounded him at the studio.

Fisher the Editor

There are two themes which regularly arise in interviews and critiques of Fisher beyond his desire to create fairy tales rather than horror films – the influence of his early career as an editor and his Christian background.

The former clearly informs many of his films, the latter's significance is disputable. There are four particular techniques that Fisher expresses which might be considered his 'signature':

1. The zoom/track and fast/slow shock aesthetic – Fisher often uses a slow pan and track such as in the opening of *Dracula* to traverse spatial boundaries as the camera appears to seamlessly move through levels of the castle into the Count's crypt. However, he also adopts infrequent, but sudden changes in pace and style of movement in order to create shocking moments, such as the reveal of the Creature in *The Curse of Frankenstein*.

2. The graphic match – Used to allude to the Gothic doppelgänger, thus subtly revealing the ambiguity in characters that might otherwise appear good. This can be seen in *Dracula* when Fisher cuts between a tight close-up of Van Helsing to the Count looking over Lucy. This cut illustrates the battle between the two powers, both fighting for total dominance; but also suggests a flimsy liminality between good and evil. Who is Van Helsing? And why does he know so much about vampires? He is on the periphery of society like the Count.

Fisher's suspenseful editing in The Two Faces of Dr Jekyll

3. Suppressing information through framing, close-ups and movement – In *The Curse of Frankenstein*, when Frankenstein leaves to retrieve the eyes, Fisher uses a close-up of The Baron's small black purse as he leaves the house. Then a close-up of

feet as he walks down the road, followed by a close-up of a coffin on which he places his bag. The exchange of the eyes happens in close-up without revealing the face of Frankenstein or the Undertaker thus the spectator's attention is sustained on the repulsive, grotesque human eyes. This technique is also used to great effect in *The Two Faces of Dr Jekyll* when Henry first drinks his potion. A close-up of 'success' written in Henry's book is followed by a wide shot of him walking to the back of the room and taking his jacket and coat (all of the time he has his back to the camera). Then there is a cut to him walking outside, once again with his back to the camera. Finally the horrific punchline is revealed in a close-up – Henry has transformed into Hyde.

4. The sustained master shot – This is perhaps the technique for which Fisher has been most criticised, yet it is one of his most effective. In *The Curse of Frankenstein* the master shot during the breakfast scene creates a particularly sinister, banal atmosphere. The Baron has just had his maid killed by the Creature, but joyfully sits for breakfast with Elizabeth. Despite the distance between spectator and action, one cannot help but stare at the red thread around her neck emanating a subtle sense of the horrific. This technique clearly influenced other Hammer directors, such as John Gilling, with *The Gorgon* and *The Reptile* particularly.

Fisher and Religion

Much has been made of Fisher's background as a Christian scientist, particularly by Paul Leggett (2002), a pastor and Hammer fan. However, as Ringel argues, religious themes and values are more prominent in the Universal horror films. He states 'accident alone bars the success of Cushing's near-miss experiments; whereas deep religio-philosophical roots foredoom Clive's gropings in the dark which is "best left unknown"' [referring to Universal's *Frankenstein* (Dir. James Whale, 1931)] (1973: 11). Fisher's Baron does all he can to deceive others in an attempt to keep his Creature alive, destroying it reluctantly, while, Universal's Henry Frankenstein has a moral crisis and realises he must destroy the Monster; he is proactive in leading the townsfolk in the witch hunt and heroically tries to defeat it alone. Henry Frankenstein seeks redemption for his actions, and upon realising the errors of his way he is rewarded by marrying Elizabeth in a restoration of social order. Hammer's Baron Frankenstein, however, is sentenced to be hanged, and even in his final days he is more obsessed with recognition for his scientific discovery than he is interested in any redemption or expressing remorse, despite calling a priest to his cell.

Morality is clearly a crucial theme in Fisher's Hammer films, despite asserting 'immorality isn't a particularly Christian thing'. He has claimed not 'to be very much of a Christian' (1964: 8). This statement questions notions that his films are deeply rooted in religious values. Fisher also explains that he would have been interested in exploring more foreign myths (in Ringel, 1973: 13) and indeed does so with *The Mummy*, *The Stranglers of Bombay* and *The Phantom of the Opera*. Fundamentally, G.R. Parfitt states, Fisher was concerned with 'the supremacy of good over evil' (1974: 54) and acknowledged 'evil is superficially a very attractive thing' (1974: 58). Fisher clearly understood this as an idea that transcends Christian values. Ultimately Fisher's films are about the human condition, and his period sets and adult fairy tales create a space where the ambiguity of the individual's goodness can be explored and examined. While evil eventually fails in all of his films, this is not always the fault of the evil-doer, as in the case of Frankenstein, where the interruptions of others is often the reason his experiments are destroyed. This is beautifully summed up by Henry in the opening of *The Two Faces of Dr Jekyll* when he explains that every man has two forces inside of him battling for supremacy: 'man as he could be' and 'man as he would be'. He desires to move beyond restrictive concepts of moral frameworks, beyond a binary opposite of good and evil. Such ambiguity is revealed through Fisher's doppelgängers: the imperialists and the Thuggees (in *The Stranglers of Bombay*), Dracula and van Helsing (and any of the many other characters who replace the latter), Frankenstein and his Creature, Leon and the beast he becomes in *The Curse of the Werewolf*, and Mocata and Duc de Richleau in *The Devil Rides Out* (Dir. Terence Fisher, 1968). This trope is also present in his earlier Hammer film *Four-Sided Triangle*. The doppelgänger trope seems more prominent in Fisher's Hammers than others.

The auteur policy enables a discussion of Fisher's particular contributions to the studio's oeuvre, which we have seen went some way to establishing the specifics of the Hammer style which would come to be recognised by fans. The foregrounding of moral ambiguity and the human condition, and panache for suspenseful editing distinguish Fisher's work from that of many of Hammer's other directors. While some of his techniques were adopted in later films, Fisher was much responsible for creating this specific, colourful style of Gothic film-making. While Fisher worked as part of a close-knit collaborative, his style was clearly recognised by Anthony Hinds as appropriate for the Hammer brand and his involvement with the studio identifies him as one of the most important directors in the history of British horror. While Pirie (2008) and Parfitt (1974) attempt to elevate Fisher to auteur status, as we have seen from a critique of the auteur policy, this isn't necessary. Whether a director considers himself a 'hack' or is hailed an auteur, a close study of his style is still useful and informative. Fisher's work not only influenced later Hammer directors, but other films, such as *The Witchfinder General* and *Count Yorga, Vampire* (Dir. Ben Kelljan, 1970).

References

Bazin, A. (1985). 'On the *politique des auteurs*', in Hillier, J. (ed.). *Cahiers du Cinema: The 1950s: Non-Realism, Hollywood, New Wave.* London & Melbourne: Routledge, pp148-258.

Benjamin, W (1968). *Illuminations.* New York: Harcourt Brace & World.

Chabrol, C. (1985). 'Rear Window', in Hillier, J. (ed.). *Cahiers du Cinema: The 1950s: Non-Realism, Hollywood, New Wave.* London & Melbourne: Routledge, pp136-139.

Comolli, J-L. et al. (1985.) 'Twenty Years On: A Discussion about American Cinema and the *politique des auteurs*', in Hillier, J. (ed.). *Cahiers du Cinema: The 1960s: New Wave, New Cinema, Re-evaluating Hollywood.* London & Melbourne: Routledge, pp196-204.

Forshaw, B. (2013). *British Gothic Cinema.* Basingstoke & New York: Palgrave Macmillan.

Hutchings, P. (2001). *Terence Fisher.* London & New York: Manchester University Press.

Jensen, P.M. (1996). 'Terence Fisher', in *The Men Who Made the Monsters*. London: Prentice Hall International, pp155-233.

Kael, P. (1963). 'Circles and Squares', in *Film Quarterly* v16 n3, pp12.26.

Kingsley, W. (1999). 'HAMMER – THE DIRECTORS', in *The House that Hammer Built* n10, pp91-94.

- ((2007). *Hammer Films: The Elstree Studio Years*. Sheffield: Tomahawk Press.

Legget, P. (2002). *Terence Fisher: Horror, Myth and Religion*. Jefferson & London: McFarland.

Moullet, L. (1985). 'Sam Fuller: In Marlowe's Footsteps', in Hillier, J. (ed.). *Cahiers du Cinema: The 1950s: Non-Realism, Hollywood, New Wave*. London & Melbourne: Routledge, pp145-157.

Murphy, R. (1992). *Sixties British Cinema*. London: BFI.

Parfitt, G.R. (1974). 'The Fruitation of Terence Fisher', in *Little Shoppe of Horrors* n3, February 1974, pp49-62.

Pirie, D. (2008). *A New Heritage of Horror*. London & New York: I.B. Tauris.

Ringel, H. (1973). 'The Horrible Hammer Films of Terence Fisher', in *Take One* v3 n9, pp8-13.

- (1975). 'Terence Fisher: The Human Side', in *Cinefantastique* v4 n3, pp1-39.

Rivette, J. (1985i). 'The Essential', in Hillier, J. (ed.). *Cahiers du Cinema: The 1950s: Non-Realism, Hollywood, New Wave*. London & Melbourne: Routledge, pp132-135.

- (1985ii). 'The Hand', in Hillier, J. (ed.). *Cahiers du Cinema: The 1950s: Non-Realism, Hollywood, New Wave*. London & Melbourne: Routledge, pp140-144.

- (1985iii). 'The Genius of Howard Hawks', in Hillier, J. (ed.). *Cahiers du Cinema: The 1950s: Non-Realism, Hollywood, New Wave*. London & Melbourne: Routledge, pp126-131.

Rohmer, E. (1985). 'Discovering America', in Hillier, J. (ed.). *Cahiers du Cinema: The 1950s: Non-Realism, Hollywood, New Wave*. London & Melbourne: Routledge, pp88-93.

Sarris, Andrew 'Notes on the Auteur Theory in 1962', in *Film Comment* v6 n3, pp7-9.

Wollen, P. (2000). 'The *auteur* theory', in Hollows, J. et al. (ed.). *The Film Studies Reader*. London: Arnold, pp71-78.

CHAPTER 5: HAMMER AFTER THE 'X'

The success of *The Quatermass Xperiment*, despite, or because of its X rating, enabled Hammer to test the BBFC's boundaries of taste. Correspondence between the censor and Hammer illustrate the studio's desire to shock audiences, while still ensuring films received a certificate. Their move into colour enhanced the shock appeal and distinguished Hammer's works from earlier cinematic reincarnations of gothic characters. The following readings of *X the Unknown* and *The Curse of Frankenstein* consider the impact of the X certificate and colour on production, and examine how these two films represent a transitional period in the studio's history, establishing many of the tropes that would appear in the studio's classic films.

X the Unknown

Director: Joseph Losey & Leslie Norman
Year of Release: 1956 Running Time: 81 minutes Certificate: X

> Here is hokum unabashed, racily put together for the delight of the millions with an appetite for the modern vein of fantastic fiction. (*The Daily Film Renter*, 1956: 3)

Synopsis: *During a routine radioactivity drill, an army platoon discovers a fissure in the ground. Soon two of the soldiers are badly affected by radiation burns and one dies. Dr Adam Royston investigates the area, discovering that the levels of radioactivity have fallen dramatically. Later that night, two young boys explore the nearby marshes. One encounters a mysterious force and, like the soldiers, he receives radiation burns and dies. In the hospital a radiographer seeks a private moment with his lover in the radiation room, where he too is affected, flesh melting from his face. Royston concludes that the organism must adapt its molecular structure and, modifying theories of evolution, presumes it is an intelligent force from the Earth's core seeking resources on the surface. Scientist Peter Elliot descends into the fissure to explore it and is nearly attacked by the organism. As it grows in size and threatens the entire town, the citizens seek refuge in the local church whilst Royston prepares to capture the creature.*

As mentioned in Chapter One, Hammer had not always produced horror films, and while the introduction of the X certificate in 1951 did not spur a sudden change in direction, it certainly assisted the studio's shift towards the genre. While most studios tried to avoid the dreaded X rating, Exclusive took the risk of exploiting it when the BBFC awarded the rating to their film adaptation of the BBC science fiction series *The Quatermass Xperiment* (Hearn & Barnes, 2007: 17) and it paid off. Despite scepticism among exhibitors about the certificate, it was hailed by some as a long needed intervention to allow more adult content to be screened. Steven Chibnall (2012) notes that in 1946 film critic Roger Manvell complained:

> It is intolerable that all films for public exhibition should be measured by the standards of the culturally under-privileged, for by such standards, if applied to great literature, a large measure of the world's masterpieces would have to be bowdlerised or abandoned. (in Chibnall, 2012: 34)

Manvell's criticism was heeded by the BBFC, which established a committee to review censorship practices. The Wheare Committee's 1950 report suggested replacing the H (Horror) category with a new X certificate, introduced in January 1951. As *Today's Cinema* explained, it was to be 'applied to films which are wholly adult in theme or treatment, and from which children under sixteen should be excluded' (1950: 34). Chibnall argues that a certain moral expectation was, however, still presumed of X rated films. At first, the certificate was primarily attributed to 'art house' foreign films (2013: 35) and was intended to allow films with adult themes to be screened in cinemas, without promoting sadistic or pornographic content. Arthur Watkins, Secretary of the BBFC emphasised this, when he explained X films were not to be 'merely sordid films dealing with unpleasant subjects, but films which, while not being suitable for children, are good adult education' (in Cornich, 1998: 24). Some exhibitors were suspicious of the new certificate however, concerned that such films would exclude a large percentage of their audience. To some extent, the X rating was perceived to be un-commercial, and James Carreras pleaded, unsuccessfully, with the BBFC (in a letter dated 26th March 1957) to resubmit *X the Unknown* for an A certificate in order to widen its distribution.

X the Unknown was Hammer's second X certified film and shot in black-and-white, and, like *The Quatermass Xperiment*, it played on its rating in its title. X the Unknown marks a transitional point in Hammer's development (as Hearn and Barnes (2007) identify) – while it can be considered a science fiction film, it clearly exhibits Gothic traits which persist in Hammer's later works. The film emphasises Cold War fears about the nuclear threat, and it is this context which enables its Gothic aesthetic – for example darkness is necessary for the Unknown's glow to resonate so effectively. Not only does the film express a Gothic look, it encourages an appropriate spectatorial relationship, with excess and abjection at the forefront of the visual and aural experience. It was the X certificate that enabled Hammer to produce this new type of body horror. While the studio's later films include iconic monsters, for much of *X the Unknown*, the camera actually expresses the point-of-view of the monster, hiding its form from view.

With the post-war hiatus of horror films, one can suspect that *X the Unknown* would not have received a certificate at all if the X rating had not been well established by the time of its release. However, this did not mean it was easily accepted by the BBFC. One reader's report declares concern that people will 'certainly have been sick' after watching this film and calls for 'more restraint'; and a letter from the BBFC to Hammer (dated 4th December, 1955) explains that while the story is suitable for certification, much of the detail is 'too nauseating' for the X category. The film's visceral horror is still notable today, and is somewhat echoed, in colour, in later films such as *Dracula*, for example when the Count's body dissolves in sunlight. Like *Quatermass* before it, *X the Unknown* expresses the human body itself as site of horror, more than focusing on an alien monster. While Hammer's later films would be defined by their monsters, the flesh as site of abject possibility would continue to dominate the visual violence of the studio's horror. The actual appearance of Hammer's monsters is rarely terrifying; in fact, in *The Gorgon* and *The Reptile*, they are quite disappointing.

To create these sites of abjection, Hammer relied on a creative special effects make-up team led by Phil Leakey, and later Roy Ashton, during its classical period. In relation to *X the Unknown*, Hearn & Barnes explain:

Make-up supervisor Phil Leakey's 'melting head' effect was achieved by taking a moulding of actor Neil Hallett's head, casting it in two halves of paraffin wax, and placing this over a plaster skull with heating elements inside. This, and the disintegration of the hapless security guard, would prove more impressive than the gelatinous Unknown itself. Much of the film's suspense was generated in anticipation of its anticlimactic unveiling. (2007: 19)

On one hand, suspense drives the film. On the other, the putrid images of dissolving flesh held in close-up foreground the Gothic and horror aesthetic which would come to dominate the Hammer oeuvre.

It was Jimmy Sangster, employed as a production manager for Hammer at the time and the film's screenwriter (his first of many writing projects for the studio), who envisioned the idea of a threat that came from within the Earth rather than outer space. The concept was initially considered because it would reduce production costs and was intended to continue from *Quatermass*, though the studio was not given permission to use the series' protagonist for this project (ibid.). However, this threat also points to Cold War paranoia and informs the film's Gothic aesthetic.

Cold War Gothicism - the nuclear wasteland in X the Unknown

In the film's opening the army sergeant and his team carry out their drill in a barren landscape. Later, the Unknown's radioactivity instigates a power blackout. Both these scenes express the Gothic theme of isolation. Thus the town, which unlike Hammer's later films is a typical 1950s environ, is thrust back into the dark ages. The Gothic themes are further illuminated when the townspeople seek refuge in the church. Here, the conflict between good and evil is expressed as good symbolised by the Christian community and evil by the nuclear-emitting creature from Earth's interior (which one can easily interpret as representing the corruption of contemporary man or the Communist threat). As one of the residents hurries people inside, he is framed between the old architecture of the church and two gravestones, ominously predicting a potential future for those in the area and reminding us of the liminality between good and evil, and life and death.

When the two young boys try to examine the marshes, one of them proceeds with caution through the wooded environ, the trees looming over and branches invading the space like an entangled spider's web. Ominous, discordant music plays a repeating motif with high pitched strings which builds tension and creates an uneasy atmosphere before the boy's horrified face, only half-lit, is revealed in close-up. He sees something off-screen (to which we are never privy). We hear a gurgling, bubbling sound emanate from the ground and he immediately runs away. The incident is never properly explained by Royston, and the boy's parents scold him for being a scientist rather than a medical doctor (thus, in their eyes, being part of the problem, meddling with science, rather than offering the solution). Once again, the visual and aural elements of the scene are classically Gothic, such trope locations, music and intense camera work have been repeated in numerous films from *Psycho* (Dir. Alfred Hitchcock, 1960) to *The Blair Witch Project* (Dir. Daniel Myrick & Eduardo Sánchez, 1999).

While accepting the many parallels and cross-contamination of science fiction and horror, Barry Langford distinguishes them in the following way:

> In the [science fiction] universe [...] the appearance of aliens, monsters and other destructive or malevolent forces is not only depicted as explicable according to the scientific understanding diegetically available (which may or may not map onto our own), but moreover is narratively subject to such analysis, explanation and - more often than not - systematic response. (2005: 164)

He continues to justify *Frankenstein* as horror rather than science fiction because the Monster's erroneous brain is not presented 'as a scientific problem but as a terrifying monstrosity' (ibid.). *X the Unknown*, however, could be considered a hybrid. Once the scientific anomaly (the radioactive fissure) has been discovered, there is a cut to Royston's workplace,

Lochmouth's Atomic Energy Establishment. The mise-en-scène of the space is typical of 1950s science fiction, lab coat-laden scientists occupy a large, bare, pale room. The decor includes strange, scientific machines, the functions of which are never explained (apart from the fact they are capable of 'testing' radioactive material). In this exposition, the aesthetics suggest science fiction. In relation to Langford's generic conventions, Royston offers a scientific theory which he uses to inform his attack on the Unknown. However, as even other characters note, the introduction to his theory is somewhat juvenile (and from there, the only advancement he makes is to apply the human condition of evolution to the Earth itself). There is little evidence of well-reasoned science here.

It is not only the look of the film which identifies it as distinctly Gothic; it also uses cinematography to create the gothic mood. The film begins with a prolonged tracking shot, with an ethereal camera moving through bare terrain. As the credits finish, the diegetic but as yet, off-screen noise of a Geiger counter starts. The hums and hisses of machines dominate the soundscape throughout the testing scene creating a nauseating feeling, which provokes a sensation of the abject, as well as reminding spectators of Cold War paranoia. It instantly encourages spectators to feel on-edge and uneasy; sensations which are further provoked by Leakey's shocking visual effects later in the film. A similar, but more intense noise emanates from Royston's machines in the film's finale. Interestingly, it is not the Unknown's presence which threatens us here, but the disturbing, relentless drone created by the machine. There is a subtle implication that we should question what we consider to be monstrous in the film, just as the young boy's parents assume the scientist might be problematic (though he assures his comrades that his intentions have always been to fix the world's issues). If we desire for the machine to be terminated, so that it is silenced, more than we care whether the creature is destroyed, are we assuming man-made nuclear technology is the real danger? Such a question was particularly significant during the height of the Cold War era.

The invasive feel of the opening soundscape is brought to a climax through the revelation of increasing degrees of radioactive burns. When Royston investigates the soldier's injuries, the audience is shown the scars on the Lancy's back. At first his sergeant lifts his arm (upon which hangs his coat) and it seems he will mask our view, but he soon moves, revealing the gruesome wounds that have mutated the soldier. Once more, in the hospital we are privy to the revelation of a patient's burns; we see the warped, plasticised surface of his skin making it seem alien, grotesque and abject. The climax comes when the radiographer is attacked. As the camera moves towards him revealing the growing intensity of his fright, its closeness feels as if it will provoke a cut to black (we might expect the horror to happen off-screen); however, there is a jarring cut to his thumb which grows and mutates. Then, a cut back to his face and we watch in horror as his features and skin melt away. The nauseating soundtrack and images of flesh reminds us of our own corporeal fragility.

When the radiographer dies, it is the intensity of the camera's movement that helps establish the tense atmosphere which culminates in his grotesque death. Unlike Hammer's later films, the camera here plays the role of the monster. The film's subjective camera has been commended by reviewers for creating an intelligent and imaginative tense atmosphere perhaps less apparent in Hammer's classic horror films (Fangoria, 1999: 35). This adds an ethereal presence to the film which parallels the opening shot (and thus encourages us to consider if our initial point-of-view was that of the Unknown). After the deliberate suspense created throughout the film, many reviewers felt let down by the Unknown's appearance: 'The sensation-seekers may be slightly disappointed by the shape adopted by the Unknown, which resembles nothing so much as a stream of very dirty oil' (Daily Film Renter, 1956: 3). Monthly Film Bulletin refers to the creature as 'a type of rolling rubber mattress, disappointingly unhorrific in content and appearance' (1956: 128). Its sloppy and awkward demeanour is perhaps more laughable than frightening, somewhat ruining the tense, Gothic atmosphere sustained until the creature's reveal. From The Curse of Frankenstein, Hammer would focus predominantly on creatures with a relatively human-form, thus combating X the Unknown's major flaw. Hammer has always been more successful with human-esque monsters. The studio's attempts at animalistic evil, such as the bats in the later Dracula films and Kiss of the Vampire (Dir. Don Sharp, 1963) and the spider in The Devil Rides Out have not aged well. It seems technological and budgetary limitations would not allow for a convincing Unknown derived from the Earth's mud.

The Curse of Frankenstein

Director: Terence Fisher
Year of Release: 1957 Running Time: 82 minutes Certificate: X

> A genuine novelty of its day – all that blood, in colour! (Hearn and Barnes, 2007: 24)

Synopsis: *Baron Frankenstein awaits his execution and summons a priest. Rather than repent his sins, he tells the Priest of his discovery and his story.*

After the death of his mother, young Victor Frankenstein hires Paul Krempe as a live-in tutor. Paul helps Victor advance his scientific interest and soon the two are working together on experiments. However, Paul becomes worried when Victor explains his desire to create a human being and begins procuring body parts. Meanwhile, Victor's love life is fraught as he is stuck between his cousin, and soon to be wife, Elizabeth who moves into his home after her parents' death, and his housemaid Justine, with whom he has been having an affair, and who believes the Baron will marry her. Though Paul worries about leaving Victor's cousin Elizabeth alone with the obsessive scientist, he cannot be involved in what he perceives as immoral work and leaves. Victor murders the renowned Professor Bernstein in order to give his creation the perfect brain, but after it is damaged during a scuffle with Paul, the Creature is devoid of intellect. Victor attempts to train it, but it escapes and kills innocent people. When Justine discovers Victor is to marry Elizabeth, she threatens to tell people about the Creature; desperate to keep his discovery secret Victor locks his maid in the lab for the Creature to kill. Eventually the Creature escapes and destroys Victor's pre-wedding party. In a showdown on the roof of his mansion, Victor accidentally shoots at Elizabeth, before he eventually destroys his creation by setting it on fire.

When Paul and Elizabeth arrive at Frankenstein's cell he implores them to confirm his story to the Priest, but they do not. He is considered a madman before he is marched to the guillotine.

Hammer's first Frankenstein film particularly distinguishes itself from earlier screen incarnations of Shelley's novel, such as Universal's *Frankenstein* and Edison's *Frankenstein's Monster* (Dir. J. Searle Dawley, 1910) because it was shot in colour. However, while Hearn and Barnes above emphasise the film's 'blood' in 'colour', it actually shows little of the former (Fisher in Ringel, 1975: 22) - a trait Fisher protests is common across his classic Hammer films. Blood is only shown three times significantly: from the original body Frankenstein retrieves, on the Creature's face when Paul shoots him, and then on Elizabeth's chest when Frankenstein accidentally shoots her. However, the colour red dominates the screen throughout, not only pre-empting the impending threat of the Creature but also creating an atmosphere which is ever-tense for the spectator. The horror comes less from the Creature, who is not to blame for his actions, or blood, but more from the imposing use of colour.

However, *The Curse of Frankenstein* was not originally intended to be a colour film. As Hearn and Barnes contest:

> The first British horror film to be made in colour was initially envisaged as a cheap black-and-white production to feature the ageing Boris Karloff, faded star of Universal's great horror cycle of the thirties. These plans stalled when Universal, who had been alerted to the company's plans by their registration of the title, raised the prospect of a lawsuit against the company should their picture contain any elements, textual or otherwise, unique to their movies. (2007:22)

Fisher claims that he never even saw the Universal films and that Hammer's version was influenced more by the novel than any earlier cinematic representation. However, the threat of a copyright lawsuit from a large Hollywood film studio overshadowed much of the filmmaking process. The final film, sans classic Hollywood star, with a flashback narrative structure, a focus on the humanity of the characters and the use of colour certainly ensured Hammer's film was distinct from Universal's. The Creature (not Monster, as Universal had it) also had to look different. In the documentary *Greasepaint and Gore* (Dir. Russell Wall, 2004), Phil Leakey recalls Hinds's frequent interruptions as he ensured the make-up effects would not mimic the Hollywood Monster.

The original script was developed by Amicus, who would later become Hammer's main horror rival. At this stage, Amicus only had one feature film in their back catalogue. After approaching Eliot Hayman and David Stillman at Associated Artists Pictures (APP), New York, Amicus was told it was too risky for them to produce a film version of the great Gothic novel because the studio lacked experience. However, APP suggested passing the script to Carreras. From the outset Michael Carreras was cautious about adapting Frankenstein, aware Hammer might have to deal with a lawsuit from Universal, but Amicus's Max J. Rosenberg assured him the script had been checked for similarities. Eventually Carreras abandoned the weak Amicus script and asked Jimmy Sangster to re-write an adaptation, but Universal were already aware of the project and Hammer's lawyers were contacted to ensure their version was distinct. The studio successfully avoided a lawsuit. Hammer's Frankenstein contrasted Universal's by being a particularly British affair; for example, the sordid inter-class affair between the Baron and his maid introduces themes of repressed passion typical of English cinema. Hammer's version also emphasises the humanity and emotions of the characters, sexual tension and violence, all heightened by the use of colour. While Marcus K. Harmes (2015) discusses the adaptation from novel to British horror film at length, one of the film's lesser considered elements is the effect of colour.

From the opening text of the film, which introduces the legend of Baron Frankenstein in sleek, red gothic font, the shocking effect of the blood red colour is apparent. The harsh, angular edges of the font complemented by the colour seem to invade the next sequence of the scenic alpine environment, attacking its peacefulness and purity. The period setting of the film is established by the grey and brown palette used in the establishing shot of the mountains and the following sequence of the prison. Such colours help to express a sense of antiquity, and this is a particular quality of Hammer's Gothic because it associates the Victorian era with superstition and myth, and expresses that these films are escapist fantasies. Thus antiquity is an important asset of the verisimilitude. Hammer would produce only a few horror films that were not period pieces, most notably *Dracula A.D. 1972*, widely considered a low point for the studio.

Colour has long been related to cinematic realism (Natalie Kalmus, 2006; Richard Barsam & David Monahan, 2010: 211), particularly since the introduction of colour celluloid. *The Curse of Frankenstein* acknowledges this as the flashback begins and the young Baron's social status is clearly exhibited through the colours of his clothes and environs. His blue jacket is a subtle, restrained tone and is accompanied by a brown waistcoat that one might expect of an older man of the time. The vibrant green wreaths expressing his mother's death are emphasised by the dim surroundings and the black attire of the funeral guests. Their beauty and vibrancy offers an aesthetic contrast with the mess of a Creature, Frankenstein later creates. The interior of the Frankenstein mansion is adorned in greys, gold, greens, whites and browns, evidence of the family's sophistication – there is nothing gaudy here.

However, *The Curse of Frankenstein* seems also to recall the dominant use of colour in early cinema. While it is popular to refer to early films as black-and-white, many colouring techniques existed during the 'primitive' era of film history. Film stock could be tinted with washes of colour, or intricately painted by hand. Colour washes were used to emphasise particular emotions and to provoke specific affect; for example, green might be used to express envy, red to express passion or rage. In *The Curse of Frankenstein*, and many subsequently Hammer films, red plays a dominant role in stimulating particular emotional responses. Fisher notes that in the scene in which the Creature attacks the child:

> I can remember painting leaves or twigs red because I wanted to foreground a suggestion of red. If people were conscious of it I don't know. The leaves' red indicating danger and the blood of the little boy went away and disappeared and you were left there staring at that little foreground of foliage with blotches of red in it. [...] This is picture making, the hidden meanings. (in Kinsley, 1997: 95)

While Fisher attributes his use of colour to creating meaning, implying here the violence toward the child, to only think about colour's representational values is reductive.

Changes in colour intensity can also provoke affect for the spectator. Silvan S. Tomkins (1995) understands 'affect' as levels of intensity felt by the body. He discusses affects such as laughter, joy, distress, anger, interest, fear and startle as part of a complex continuum defined by 'simulation increase, simulation level and simulation decrease' (1995: 46). He distinguishes these affects by density and intensity of the neural firing which provokes them. Strong reactions to colour may provoke such neural changes as spectators relate to new visual intensities. Paul Coates (2010) suggests colour intensity not only relates to its place on the spectrum – scientifically and psychologically – but also its purity. He claims red, blue, yellow and green in their primary form are more intense than mixed colours (2010: 9). Sudden changes in the intensity of colour – in terms of their shade, frequency and purity – in a film can be greatly affective. The lurid primary red in *The Curse of the Frankenstein* is constantly foregrounded and shapes the spectatorial relationship with the film.

The film experience always has an extra-diegetic dimension – the relationship between film and audience, a facet of which Fisher seemed deeply aware with his tense camera movement and vibrant colours. While red can symbolise danger and death, it also creates a subjective perspective of the diegetic environs. The stark colour contrasts highlight that this is not to be taken as an objective, realist image. However, this colouring does not necessarily encourage spectators to align themselves with a specific character's point-of-view. Rather, it implies the particular way the spectator should feel watching such sequences, evoking sensations of horror, anticipation and fear. This is particularly noticeable in sequences when there is no imminent danger (though it is never far away). For example, when Elizabeth and Victor have breakfast, she wears a red ribbon around her neck. The vibrancy of her adornment counteracts the verisimilitudinous colour palette of the Frankenstein mansion, and we are drawn to its vividness. The lure of the colour creates anticipation as the spectator waits with bated breath for the next moment of horror. The fact Hammer submitted the film in black-and-white to the censors suggests the producers were all too aware of the powerful effect of its colours.

While the use of colour is particularly poignant and affective in *The Curse of Frankenstein*, due to colour degrading the true potential effect of this is sadly lost. As Barry Forshaw notes, 'modern audiences have to use a certain imagination, mentally filling in the rich colours of the film which were so much a part of its original shocking effect on audiences' (2013: 40). Fortunately the cinematic experience always provokes our imagination, thus if modern spectators imagine what it must have been like to see colour for the first time in a horror film, then hopefully the effect that encouraged so many critics to be outraged and shocked by this work can be understood.

References

Barsam, R. & Monahan, D. (2013). *Looking at Movies: Introduction to Film*. New York & London: W. W. Norton & Company.

Chibnall, S. (2012). 'From the Snake Pit to the Garden of Eden: A Time of Temptation for the Board', in Lamberti, E. (ed.). *Behinds the Scenes at the BBFC: Film Classification from the Silver Screen to the Digital Age*. London: Palgrave Macmillan.

The Cinema (1956). 'X the Unknown' review. 15th August, p9.

Coates, P. (2010). 'Colour and Suffering', in *Cinema and Colour: The Saturated Image*. London: Palgrave Macmillan.

Cornich, I. (1998). 'X Films', in *Sight and Sound* v8 n5, pp24-26.

The Daily Film Renter (1956). 'X the Unknown' review. 16th August, p3.

Fangoria (1999). 'X the Unknown (Anchor Bay)' review. July, p35.

Forshaw, B. (2013). *British Gothic Cinema*. Basingstoke: Palgrave Macmillan.

Harmes, M. K. (2015). *The Curse of Frankenstein*. Leighton Buzzard: Auteur.

Hearn, M. & Barnes, A. (2007). *The Hammer Story: The Authorised History of Hammer Film*. London: Titan Books Ltd.

Kalmus, N. (2006). 'Colour Consciousness', in Vacche, A. & Price, B. (ed.). *Colour: The Film Reader*. New York & London: Routledge.

Kinsley, W. (1997). 'The Curse of Frankenstein', in *The House that Hammer Built* n1, pp44-56.

Langford, B. (2005). 'The Horror Film', in *Film Genre: Hollywood and Beyond*. Edinburgh: Edinburgh University Press, pp158-181.

Monthly Film Bulletin (1956). 'X the Unknown' review. October, p128.

Ringel, H. (1975). Terence Fisher: The Human Side', in *Cinefantastique* v4 n3, pp1-10, 15-18 & 19-39.

Today's Cinema (1950). 'New Year Brings 'X' Certificate'. 13th December, pp2 and 34.

Tomkins, S. S. (1995). *Exploring Affect: The Selected Writing of Silvan S. Tomkins*. Demos, E. V. (ed.). Cambridge: Cambridge University Press.

CHAPTER 6: CLASSIC HAMMER BEYOND FRANKENSTEIN

The success of *The Curse of Frankenstein* encouraged a succession of Hammer horror productions, the most profitable of which were produced between 1957 and 1966. Kinsley contests that there is much dispute about what constitutes Hammer's 'classical period'. Some argue that it starts with *The Quatermass Xperiment* in 1955 and ends with the flop *The Phantom of the Opera* in 1962. Others believe it ends with the move from Bray in 1966 (Kinsley, 2008: 6). This latter definition is more inclusive and recognises the diversity of Hammer's film-making during the Bray Studios years, when the majority of the team were regulars and came to define a particular Hammer style, which began to disintegrate as productions moved to Elstree and sex and nudity became more prominent themes. The following case study readings focus on particular traits of the classic films, including the Gothic doppelgänger, the representation of women and Hammer's vampire mythology.

The Stranglers of Bombay

Director Terence Fisher
Year of Release 1959 Running Time 80 minutes Certificate A

> The Hammer boys have gone all out here to supply a full measure of Grand Guignol horror thrills, with robbery, murder, torture and killings galore. (*The Daily Cinema*, 1959: 5)

Synopsis: *India 1826. New recruits of the Thuggees swear allegiance to the goddess Kali and are offered the sacred silk white cloth.*

The British East India Company has become aware of thousands of cargo disappearances. The experienced, but homesick, Captain Lewis has started to solve the mysteries and hopes to be given the responsibility officially. However, he discovers the under-qualified and ignorant officer Connaught-Smith has been offered the position. Lewis's servant Ram Das is murdered by his, now Thuggee, brother spurring the Captain to combat the cult. In his quest, Lewis is beaten. He tries to express his concerns that a murderous cult is behind the disappearances, but he is ignored and finally dismissed from the company. Even after being kidnapped by the cult, he fails to persuade others of the threat. The company's caravan is ambushed, and Connaught-Smith and his companions murdered. Lewis comes face-to-face with the High Priest, who, with the help of Ram Das's brother, he is able to defeat.

The Stranglers of Bombay is now marketed as one of Hammer's adventure films and, like *The Abominable Snowman* (Dir. Terence Fisher, 1957), was shot in black-and-white. It is loosely based on real incidents, atypical for Hammer. However, its expression of the doppelgänger trope to represent fears of post-colonialism emphasises its Gothic nature, highlighting the transcendental nature of the mood that does not necessarily recognise generic boundaries (as discussed in Chapter Three). While many of Hammer's Dracula and Frankenstein films seem to be rooted in the traditions of British Gothic literary, *Stranglers*, *The Abominable Snowman* and *The Mummy* were early examples of plots influenced by non-British myths (something Fisher was always keen to explore), a trend which continued with *The Witches* (Dir. Cyril Frankel, 1966) and *The Plague of Zombies* among other films.

There was a certain truth value attributed to *Stranglers* in its production and marketing (despite their questionable accuracy). It was advertised with the tagline 'This is true! This is real! This actually happened!' and its black-and-white palette emphasised its documentary, rather than fantasy, quality. Furthermore, Fisher worked with historical expert Michael Edwards to create an authentic aesthetic (Dudley, 2002: 43). Its exotic setting (though still filmed at Bray) has determined that it be categorised as action/adventure, rather than as one of Hammer's horrors, despite its Gothic tendencies. To some extent, it foreshadows the shift in the horror genre after Hammer towards more 'realist' terror based loosely on modern legends and 'true' stories. It was influenced by the real Indian cult, the Phansigars (The Strangling Ones), more colloquially known as 'the Thuggees'. The announcement that it was to be presented in the faux-technology Strangloscope promised Hammer fans a horrific affair equivalent to *The Curse of Frankenstein* and *Dracula*, and, despite the reversion to black-and-white, Kinsley calls it 'Fisher's grimmest and most sadistic film' (1997: 111).

Stranglers was exemplary of the Carreras/horror tension. Michael pushed for a more diverse slate of films, including historical dramas like *Stranglers*, but the rest of the team managed to convert it into a horror with images of severed hands and bludgeoned eye socks: 'Hammer went all out to push the production as Hammer horror' (Dudley, 2002: 44). The BBFC recommended four minutes of cuts and once they had been satisfied the film received an A rating, rather than the X which Hammer fans had begun to expect. Despite its graphic black-and-white severed limbs, the A rating severely affected its reception.

Reviews of *Stranglers* written at the time of its release certainly suggest that it was perceived as part of the studio's horror oeuvre. *The Daily Cinema*'s (1959) review above highlights the Grand Guignol style with which Hammer was becoming commonly associated, while other magazines, such as *Variety* (1959) and *Monthly Film Bulletin* (1960) specifically comment on the film's unusual mix of a realistic aesthetic with horrific imagery. On one hand, *Variety* commended the studio, stating:

> Hammer Productions, which for some time has concentrated, with solid b.o. [box office] winnings, on horror has lately decided to grow up. True, Hammer is still delving in the horror market but current pix are not exploiting horror for the sake of it. The case of 'Stranglers of Bombay' is typical. Here is a chance to bring in a few horrific moments but, mainly, the film is a straightforward melodrama. (1959: 17)

On the other hand, it was the turn to 'realism' that *Monthly Film Bulletin* blamed for the film's particularly gruesome nature:

> In spite of, or more probably because of, its veneer of historical truth, this is a particularly bestial contribution to the Hammer horror cycle: the parallels to much more recent atrocities seem more marked than ever. The production is the usual fleabitten affair, unimaginatively unconvincing, quite without period sense, and relying almost entirely for its appeal on visual outrages - blindings, evisceration, human heads thrown on to dinner tables, and so forth- which gain if anything by being shot for once in black-and-white. (1960: 10)

Considering reviews such as this, it is not unfounded to label *Stranglers* as a 'Hammer horror'. The film is a rarity because it works against Fisher's admission that he wanted to present the horrific in a fantastical context. His decision to work on the film perhaps supports his suggestion that he was indeed a 'hack director', who didn't get to choose his work

– although in interviews, he seemed pleased to have been offered the opportunity even if he was somewhat dissatisfied with the final film (Hutchings, 2001: 104). As well as *Stranglers*, Hammer's horror style often seeped into its thrillers, such as *Scream of Fear* and *The Hound of the Baskervilles*.

Like *The Mummy*, *The Abominable Snowman*, *The Phantom of the Opera*, *The Gorgon*, *The Plague of Zombies*, *The Reptile* and *The Witches*, *Stranglers* also challenges perceptions that Hammer's horror films were always rooted in a particularly British or English Gothic. While the specificity of the aesthetics, accents and themes can be interpreted within a particular British context, these stories highlight Fisher and Hammer's interest in myths beyond British Gothic literature. *The Mummy* and *Stranglers*, among others, are given a British contextualisation however, with their clear reference to colonialism – in both films, status is related to ethnicity. As I.Q. Hunter notes, '*The Mummy* (1959) echoes... fears of imperial decline (its theme of Egyptian revenge carries unavoidable post-Suez resonances)' (2013: 41). Stranglers is even more specific in its reference to colonial guilt and post-colonial fears as it explicitly deals with the conflict between native peoples (albeit heavily stereotyped to a standard most would consider racist today) and white British authority in a country that had only been partitioned in 1947 (still recent history when the film was produced).

Peter Hutchings suggests the film expresses anxieties of difference (2001: 103). However, the Thuggee Other in *Stranglers* can also be understood as a mirror of the British subjects and such a reading seems particularly convincing when one considers the film's cultural context. The partitioning of India was a significant event in colonial history, setting a precedent for the gradual demise of the British and other European empires. At this time, more countries began to seek their freedom from old colonial ties, while Europe was attempting to recover from the devastation caused by World War Two. Britain and other European colonialists, after some initial resistance, eventually realised maintaining the old empires was no longer financially viable. In British history, therefore, the partitioning of India signifies a major political and cultural shift, a moment which triggered the nation's move from dominant world power to post-colonial nation.

While Dror Izhar (2011) dismisses the film as one which exhibits 'racist paranoia' (2011: 112) and 'one of the last films to deny decolonization' (2011: 128), read through the Gothic lens, the messages portrayed about colonialism seem far more complex. Stephen D. Arata (1996) notes the significance of colonialism to Victorian Gothic literature, particularly Bram Stoker's work. He explains that in the year *Dracula* was published, Britain's global dominance was already in decline.

> The loss of overseas markets for British goods, the economic and political rise of Germany and the United States, the increasing unrest in British colonies and possessions, the growing domestic uneasiness over the morality of imperialism – all combined to erode Victorian confidence in the inevitability of British progress and hegemony. Late-Victorian fiction in particular is saturated with the sense that the entire nation – as a race of people, as a political and imperial force, as a social and cultural power – was in irretrievable decline. (1996: 161)

Britain, which had hosted the Great Exhibition in 1851, a symbol of its important role in the new enlightened and industrial age, was already (only forty years later) starting to confront anxiety about the potential demise of its empire. During this period, Arata notes the popularity of 'reverse colonization' narratives, where foreigners would invade British land. Significantly he argues:

> But fantasies of reverse colonization are more than products of geopolitical fears. They are also responses to cultural guilt. In the marauding, invasive Other, British culture sees its own imperial practices mirrored back in monstrous forms. [...] Reverse colonization narratives thus contain the potential for powerful critiques of imperialist ideologies, even if that potential usually remains unrealized. As fantasies, these narratives provide an opportunity to atone for imperial sins, since reverse colonization is often represented as deserved punishment. (1996: 162)

Sixty years after the publication of *Dracula*, Victorian anxieties about a diminishing Empire started to become a reality with the partitioning of India. The Thuggees in *Stranglers* never leave India to threaten the British Isles, but, indeed, neither does Hammer's Dracula (until the final films of the series). However the Thuggees represent a mirroring of Imperialist criminality through the exposition of the Gothic motif, the doppelgänger.

Gothic monsters often express repressed societal fears and serve as identity mirrors, particularly presented through the doppelgänger motif. The monsters in *Stranglers* are not supernatural creatures but human cultists who explicate the anxiety of Britain's shift from colonial power to the unknown world of post-colonialism. As typical of the doppelgänger, the Thuggees behaviours are mirrored by the film's English characters, often as villainous as their monstrous counterparts. Paul Wells defines the doppelgänger as follows:

> ... effectively a 'double', in which humankind confronts its nemesis either through the opposition of an individual and a monster by the exposure of the two competing sides of an individual – normally, one rational and civilised, the other uncontrolled and irrational, often more primal and atavistic. (2003: 8)

Gothic monsters thus serve as mirrors for the subjects who attempt to confront them, highlighting the primal behaviour and attitudes in the 'good' characters who supposedly represent a moral society or one familiar to the spectator. In *Stranglers*, the tribal Thuggees are set against the Imperialist rulers. While *The Mummy* has been read as evidencing resonance of the Suez Crisis, *Stranglers* clearly represents fears about the crumbling British Empire. Though the Thuggees believe Lewis is their challenger, to his white British colleagues he is a reprobate, working outside the system. In the film, the doppelgänger motif instead pairs the Thuggee High Priest and the Imperialist Connaught-Smith, highlighting the barbaric and primitive tendencies in colonial behaviour as much as expressing such sentiment about the occult.

British Imperialist versus Thugee cult in The Stranglers of Bombay

At first glance, the Thuggee High Priest and Connaught-Smith appear to be binary opposites. The former is a man hungry with power who forces another to murder his own brother. He refuses men the opportunity to do things that benefit only themselves (blinding two men in a horrific ceremony near the opening of the film). He has no appreciation for any union that is not between the one and the Goddess, Kahli. His belief system suppresses the individual. Connaught-Smith, a man driven by reason and rule, considers himself of high social and military status (whether his opinion on these matters is accurate, he convinces others of the same). Over-ridden with rational and reasoned thinking, he refuses to listen to Lewis and instead concerns himself with banal questionings which get him nowhere and is subsequently murdered by the Thuggees.

The Thuggee High Priest is presented as a barbaric madman – half-naked, his gestures are often dramatic and somewhat primitive (at least in the history of cinematic performance, where histrionic or theatrical body language belongs to early cinema). In contrast, Connaught-Smith arrives on horse-back and wears his smartly ironed uniform with pride (appearance is clearly important to him as he criticises Lewis for looking scruffy after being attacked). However, just like the High Priest, Connaught-Smith suppresses individualism, ignoring Lewis's evidence in favour of ensuring the next shipment of goods goes ahead, so the capitalist company does not suffer. Religion and capitalism are presented not as binary opposites, but through the motif of the doppelgänger. Though the two men may appear to be different, there is an uncanny resemblance between them. Like the majority of Hammer's films, *Strangers* is ideologically ambiguous. Neither Connaught-Smith nor the Thuggee leader is virtuous or victorious. The High Priest's primitive and ritualistic behaviour is mirrored in Connaught-Smith's ignorant colonial attitude and they are both punished for their moral crimes. In some respect, the film can be seen as a celebration of individualism because only the renegade Lewis survives. Such celebration would become prominent in the 1960s 'kitchen sink' realist films against which Hammer's works are often positioned.

Lewis symbolises modern individualism. However, in many respects he resembles the hysterical Gothic woman (in the film's merchant and army context, it has to be a man). He is a man trapped abroad, expressing to his wife that he wishes to return home. He is surrounded by pompous English men who haven't bothered to learn anything about their surroundings – they use and abuse its people and environment (for which they are punished by the Thuggees). Lewis's awareness of the ignorance of his comrades expresses the guilt of the British – their refusal to listen leads them and their Indian servants (treated little better than slaves) to the slaughter. Lewis's hysterical expressions present him as a madman, such as when he runs to speak with Connaught-Smith flustered and dirty after being beaten. In exhibiting fear he is a liminal character symbolising great uncertainty about the cultural and political shift in British society, when the future of the Empire and a distinct British nationhood as Imperialist was in crisis. Like many of Hammer's hysterical characters though, such as Helen in *Dracula, Prince of Darkness*, Lewis is the most knowledgeable person in the diegesis. Unlike his female counterparts in other Hammer films, he does not come to a grisly demise, however. His ability to evaluate fairly, rather than see the world from one point of view is rewarded. Lewis is not external to the colonial threat, as Hutchings (2001) highlights, but he does provide some level of compromise, some desire for a better future, in contrast to the men who favour extreme oppression. As such, Lewis represents the fragile, liminal nature of Britishness as it shifts from colonial power to post-colonial nation.

In its final words, the film highlights this dichotomy of British fear/guilt:

> ...Major General Sir William Sleeman, the officer of the East India Company actually responsible for [the Thuggees] capture, wrote of his fellow officers: 'If we have done nothing else for India, we have done this good thing.'

The implication of guilt in the final line, 'if we have done *nothing else for India*' suggests that, overall, the presence of Britain was not a good thing for the country. Yet it also celebrates the British achievement of destroying the Thuggees. On one hand, the removal of the British from colonies such as India not only liberated the native peoples, but alleviated the British from their guilt (while also drawing attention to a history of colonial violence). On the other hand, it relinquished the British of power, thus an uncertain future lay ahead – one which provoked fear. Thus the colonial past in *Stranglers* is represented ambiguously – it is celebrated, expressed through a nostalgic lens as romantic, yet it is frightening. However, it also acknowledges the guilt the nation must bear for suppressing so many peoples and cultures.

The Gorgon

Director Terence Fisher
Year of Release 1964 Certificate X

> Old students will not be deterred by the fact that the identity of the villainess is early obvious. (Variety, 1964: 6)

Synopsis: *In the small town of Vandorf, 1910, Sascha Cass tells her city boyfriend Bruno that she is pregnant; he rushes immediately to inform her father that he will fulfil his obligations. Sascha, concerned that her father might kill her lover, chases after him. However, en route she is turned to stone. Bruno's body is discovered hanging from a tree soon after. In court, the case is dismissed as the murder of Sascha by Bruno, and his subsequent suicide. However, Bruno's father is suspicious and stays in Vandorf in search of the truth. He visits the nearby Castle Borski where he encounters the gorgon Megaera who turns him to stone. Soon Bruno's brother, Paul arrives in the village and falls in love with Carla, who appears to be involved with Dr. Namaroff. Namaroff is concerned that Megaera has taken human form.*

Paul has a near-miss encounter with the gorgon which ages him dramatically. He begs Carla to leave with him, but at first she refuses. His colleague Professor Meister arrives from Leipzig worried about the length of Paul's absence. Meister believes Carla is Megaera, but Paul refuses to admit it. Carla finally declares she is ready to leave Vandorf and Paul sends her to Leipzig, but she never arrives. In the castle, Paul, Namaroff, the Professor and Megaera face each other, and the tragic lovers never fulfil their dreams.

In Hammer's early horror films, women play minor roles. For example, in *The Curse of Frankenstein*, Elizabeth is Frankenstein's quaint fiancée, who wishes to be involved with his work only when she realises how much it distracts him. While Frankenstein has his lustful distraction, Justine, she is killed as soon as she threatens to expose his work. Both women are relatively dispensable (though Elizabeth does not die). In *The Mummy*, Isobel uses her feminine beauty to tame the reanimated mummy by releasing her hair in order to resemble Ananka, who the titular character once loved. She does not become 'phallic', a claim often made about women in horror, but instead uses her feminine beauty to control the monstrous creature. Even in *Brides of Dracula* (Dir. Terence Fisher, 1960), despite the title's suggestion of dominating evil vampiresses, women are submissive to Baron Meinster. While Hutchings (2001) argues Hammer's films are undoubtedly male-centric, it would be brash to define them as misogynistic; they do offer a heterogeneous image of femininity across the oeuvre.

Hammer's women have usually been discussed in relation to overt sexuality; Hearn's book *Hammer Glamour* (2009) celebrates the studio's beautiful female stars. Hammer's later Karnstein trilogy, or what Pirie calls 'the sex vampire' films (2008: 179), display the female body for titillation shifting from Fisher's restrained Gothic style towards lesbian soft-core pornography. However, some of the studio's 1970s films offer a more complex image of femininity. In *Countess Dracula* (Dir. Peter Sasdy, 1971) and *Captain Kronos, Vampire Hunter* (Dir. Brian Clemens, 1974), the female villains seek everlasting beauty and immortality. They drain the blood of young girls in order to remain youthful. While Lady Durward in *Kronos* is a cold, vicious killer, she resurrects her husband so they can live together eternally; and Countess Dracula is tormented by her battle for youth, becoming older each time the blood's power diminishes. To consider the representation of Hammer's women as homogeneous – as pure titillation for a male audience – is to refute the wide range of female characters the films present and to deny the pleasure that a specifically heterosexual, female audience might find watching them. *The Gorgon*, a much-neglected film in the Hammer collection, offers a particularly rich and interesting portrayal of femininity very different from much of the studio's work. Carla's body is an ambiguous site and she grapples with similar existential issues to Hammer's leading males.

One critic lambastes the film for making it obvious who the gorgon is relatively early (*Monthly Film Review*, 1964: 149). However, as the *Variety* review noted earlier recognises, this should not matter to hardened Hammer fans. Indeed, it is the conflict in Carla's identity which is crucial to the film. Barbara Creed (1993) re-reads Freud's interpretation of the gorgon myth. She identifies three central ideas in Freud's analysis: 1). Medusa's snake-hair is phallic – replacing the penis and thus emphasising the Mother's 'lack' (of a penis) as horrific; 2). When Medusa is beheaded by Perseus, her head becomes a fetish object 'confirming both the absence and presence of the mother's penis'; and 3). The act of turning to stone is a metaphor for the male erection (1993: 111). She interprets the gorgons as castrating women who possess the 'vagina dentata' (the toothed vagina), a symbol which has existed in global legends for centuries. Thus, she argues, this figure represents a threat to patriarchal society and is tamed by a male through the beheading which restores order. The gorgon, then, is what Creed calls the 'monstrous-feminine' (1993: 151) – her threat is distinctly rooted in her own sexuality, not her lack.

However, Creed's analysis here is related to the Medusa myth, it is not a specific reading of Hammer's film, and one must always be careful to consider appropriations of popular legends in light of their specific context. Sexuality is obviously a potent quality of Hammer's films. One must be wary, however, of only focusing on this dimension, for it assumes no other character qualities are significant. Carla, like many of Hammer's male leads, is a tormented, ambiguous individual. It is interesting to compare her to her male counterparts to consider the extent to which gender impinges on how she expresses similar existential crises relevant to the era and production context of Hammer's classic horror films. The majority of Hammer's films from 1957 to the mid-1970s are based in the Victorian era, when Enlightenment challenged religious superstition. They were produced during another time of great social upheaval: the Empire was collapsing, women, homosexuals and black people (among other minority groups) were beginning to call for more rights, the teenage generation was becoming more vocal, and the 'swinging Sixties' were underway, inspired by the sexual revolution. As in the Victorian era, traditional values were being re-considered.

Hutchings believes *The Gorgon* offers an unusual representation of femininity for Hammer, but that fundamentally its protagonist's agency is still limited and defined by the male gaze: 'Men look at her and then they die: she does not do anything to cause this, she just is' (2001: 135-137). However, this negates the haunting voice of Megaera that entices her victims towards the castle, a voice which hypnotises like Mocata's (*The Devil Rides Out*), and Dracula's eyes. Carla/Megaera represents the existential crisis of an individual torn between two types of being, like many of Hammer's male characters. Columbia's pressbook for the film recognises the similarity between Carla and earlier male protagonists, stating that she is as monstrous as 'Dracula, Frankenstein, the werewolf…' and 'lives a Jekyll-and-Hyde existence'. The distributor attempts to sell the film on its female monster/heroine. It would be easy to read her tension as a Christian dualism. However, Hammer's types are not this simple. Carla is not a pure young girl. Though she is somewhat suppressed by Namaroff, for her own protection, there is an implied romance between them. Once she meets a young man from the city, despite initial resistance, she desires to run away with him. She is not the pure virgin character one might position in dualism with the evil gorgon, who petrifies men. This is not dissimilar from Henry Jekyll and Edward Hyde. The former has, for all intents and purposes, abandoned his wife and is obsessed with his work, while Hyde kills Kitty Jekyll and Paul Allen (with whom she is having an affair). The evil of Hyde's actions is ambiguous because he seeks vengeance upon those who are making a fool of Henry. He seems to act on Henry's potentially repressed desires while Jekyll is hardly virtuous. Therefore, how might we understand the dualistic characters so central to Hammer's films?

Friedrich Nietzsche's philosophy offers a useful framework for evaluating such characters and Hammer's films can be read as interrogating his ideas about morality (or at least Nietzschean thought as understood by Henry Jekyll). At the beginning of *The Two Faces of Dr Jekyll*, Henry states that we all have two beings trying to fight for superiority inside us: 'man as he could be' and 'man as he would'. He is dedicated to moving beyond traditional moral thinking and the concept of a binary opposite of 'good and evil'. Nietszche argues that the 'search for truth' is doomed to fail. It is a search he believes has the potential to destroy life rather than enlighten. Alternatively, he implies the 'will to power' is the driving force for all mankind (2000). Nietzsche's übermensch is a man-beyond-man with a strong will to power (over a search for knowledge), who is

> willing to risk all for the sake of enhancement of humanity. In contrary to the last man whose sole desire is his own comfort and is incapable of creating anything beyond oneself in any form. This should suggest that an overman is someone who can establish his own values as the world in which others live their lives, often unaware that they are not pregiven. (Anon, https://ccrma.stanford.edu/~pj97/Nietzsche.htm)

The übermensch lives outside normal, rational society, but seeks to improve it; the majority of people would not understand him. Many of

Hammer's leading men can be seen as striving for the status of the übermensch – Jekyll and Frankenstein for instance – however, they ultimately fail. Nietzsche's übermensch and the last man of our time are incompatible, a problem he never resolves in his work. His übermensch inflects indefinitely upon history or can transcend it. Hyde's comment expresses a 'Hammification' of Nietzsche's idea and establishes the ethical framework at the foundation of many of the studio's horror films.

Those Hammer protagonists who do not appear to be obsessed with enhancing humanity but express a bestial identity can also be understood in this context. They represent a primal will to power – a desire to be unleashed from the world of rationality, science (or religion) and knowledge, and to possess ultimate power, but perhaps not the restraint to use this power for good – and this is the core of their struggle. Individuals like Leon (*The Curse of the Werewolf*) and Carla want so desperately to be rid of their primal will to power in order to be good, but they cannot. Carla's possessed body as Megaera is able to exert power over others, literally sucking life out of them. The conflict between Carla and Megaera, absent in the original Greek myth, represents the struggle Jekyll mentions but as 'woman as she could be' and 'women as she would be'. The former is represented in the figure of Megaera – an overpowering figure who appears, like Dracula, at the top of the staircase or from the castle's landing. When she is first revealed she is a dark figure in the shadows, then in extreme-close-up her forehead and eyes (her source of power) are shown, followed by a close-up of her face, before Paul screams in agony and stumbles out of the castle. The close-ups of her eyes, her extravagantly clothed appearance and her abode express similarities with Count Dracula; both are powerful, bourgeois figures with hypnotic superhuman powers.

The struggle, described by Jekyll, that Carla experiences between the two identities is represented in the sequence when she meets Paul in the castle. The tense, Gothic atmosphere encountered when he first visited is repeated. A figure is seen sitting atop a red and gold throne on the balcony landing. The female wears a gold and red cloak matching the environs. She seems to command the space and sounds stern as she explains, 'they won't follow me here'. For a moment, it seems he might be facing Megaera, but it is Carla. She only breaks from this powerful exposition when she explains she will leave with Paul, and passionately runs to embrace him. This is the 'woman as she would be' – one who gets to fulfil her dream of being with a man she truly loves, rather than suppressed by Namaroff. She wants the freedom to have the choice of who she will express her sexuality to, but instead her lover must behead her to destroy the Megaera curse. As with many of Hammer's leads, good cannot exist after evil is destroyed, instead both must be sacrificed. These characters are 'beyond good and evil' (to steal the title of Nietzsche's work); they represent the complexity of morality. Such expressions of morality are particularly potent during eras of great social upheaval, when ethical codes go through processes of redefinition. Hammer's protagonists, including some of the studio's women such as Carla/ Megaera represent not only crises of gender, but wider anxieties about societal change.

Carla takes her place as Megaera in The Gorgon

Nietzsche claims:

> We should not be '*merely* moral' men. Apart from morality, this faith is a stupidity that reflects little honor on us. In bourgeois life ever-present suspicion may be considered a sign of 'bad character' and hence belong among things imprudent; here, among us, beyond the bourgeois world and its Yes and No – what should prevent us from being imprudent and saying: a philosopher has nothing less than a *right* to 'bad character'. (2000: 236)

Carla, like many of Hammer's leading males, expresses a struggle between so-called 'bad' and 'good character'. The existence of both in the same body emphasises the problems with the duality of pre-existing moral systems that Nietzsche highlights. The young generation that Hammer originally spoke to in auditoriums were themselves developing new frameworks that challenged earlier systems, as during the era of Enlightenment, when growing Victorian secularism and anti-colonialist sentiment had challenged traditional religious values, issues with which the classic gothic novels of the time engaged.

While Carla's 'woman as she would be' values are traditionally feminine – ultimately she desires love – this is not unlike some of Hammer's men, such as Leon. Love is not solely a feminine characteristic in Hammer's films, even if it is often portrayed as such. However, fundamentally she grapples with a similar existential crisis as her male counterparts. We must not forget gender and sexuality, so obviously significant in Hammer's films, but we must also consider other issues that characters embody. Shifting definitions of gender were occurring as Hammer produced some of their most successful films, but was only one issue within a wider pattern of social change.

Dracula, Prince of Darkness

Year of Release 1966 Running Time 90 minutes Certificate X

> That sexy old blood-sucker is at it again! With Hammer at the helm and Christopher Lee once again baring his fangs with gleeful relish, any further comments are practically unnecessary. (*The Daily Cinema*, 1965: 8)

Synopsis: *Father Sandor interrupts the funeral of a young girl to stop the local priest's anti-vampire ritual and to allow her to have a respectable burial.*

Four middle-class English travellers – Charles Kent, his wife Diana, Charles's older brother Alan and his uptight wife Helen – visit the Carpathian Mountains on holiday. While Charles enjoys his time with the locals in a tavern, Helen disapproves. They encounter Father Sandor, the Abbot of Kleinberg who warns them not to visit the castle on Carlsbad road. The men dismiss the quirky monk believing him to be promoting his town. They head towards Carlsbad, only to find their coach driver abandoning them in the forests. A driverless carriage appears and takes them to Dracula's castle where dinner places have been laid for them, but no one is in sight. Helen grows more suspicious and Klove, Dracula's servant, helps them settle in. During the night, Alan finds himself sacrificed for the resurrection of Dracula. Helen is turned into a vampire and attempts to attack the others to the anger of Dracula. The Count proceeds to stalk the innocent Diana with the help of his servant, Ludwig. Sandor assists Charles's hunt for Dracula, but in the final showdown it is the quick thinking of Diana – who shoots at the ice on which the Count stands – that ensures their victory. Dracula drowns in the icy water.

Dracula, Prince of Darkness was Hammer's fourth vampire film, but the first *Dracula* sequel proper (*The Brides of Dracula* does not feature the Count; rather it touches on the Elizabeth Báthory legend). Though *Dracula* is the most famous of the Hammer series, *Dracula, Prince of Darkness* was the studio's first attempt at creating vampire mythology, allowing us to discuss here Hammer's specific depiction of the 'King of Vampires'.

Stoker's novel was not the first literary text about vampires, even if it is the most famous. Published in 1897, it contributed to an established genre, which included work such as *The Vampire* (John Polidori, 1819), *Varney the Vampire* (Thomas P. Prest, 1847) and *Carmilla* (Sheridan Le Fanu, 1872). The origins of the vampire on screen are much disputed. Bruce G. Hallenbeck (2010) notes, that while Georges Méliès's *Le manoir du diable* (1896) is often considered the first vampire film, 'it merely features the first example of what would become a staple of vampire films: a bat transforming into a man – in this case, Mephistopheles' (2010: 13). Furthermore serials like *Les vampires* (Louis Feuillade, 1915-16) depict criminals or 'vampish women' emphasising the rebellious and sexual undertones of the vampiric myth, but negating the supernatural qualities. The Hungarian film *Drakula halála* (*The Death of Drakula*, Károly Lajthay, 1921) may be the first screen adaptation of the Count's tale; however it has been lost and evidence suggests it borrowed the name 'Dracula' rather than portrayed vampirism (Hallenbeck, 2010: 84).

The German Expressionist film *Nosferatu* (Dir. F.W. Murnau, 1922) is therefore generally considered the first cinematic re-telling of the Dracula myth. However it was produced without the permission of Stoker's estate and, although all of the characters' names and elements of the plot were changed, the Stoker estate won a legal case and demanded that all copies of the film were destroyed (fortunately they were not and it can still be seen today). Other vampire stories followed in Europe and America, but it was Universal's 1931 *Dracula* that became the most famous pre-Hammer adaptation of the novel. Universal bought the rights to the literary work and subsequent theatrical adaptation, and thus presented the first legal screen version. Universal's Count is a decadent but strange individual – his castle looks like it has not been occupied for hundreds of years. As performed by Bela Lugosi, the Count has a Hungarian accent and represents the invasion of the foreign influence, interestingly at a time when a large number of Europeans were coming to work in Hollywood.

Hammer's *Dracula* was the first depiction of the myth in colour. The declaration 'I am Dracula' is imitated by Bernard's 'Dra-cu-la' riff in the musical score, three chords that symbolise the Count's name. However, Christopher Lee's dominating presence is countered by his gentlemanly and humble welcome, as he quickly lifts Jonathan Harker's suitcase and glides up the stairs at a supernatural speed. Lee's Dracula shifts between refined, graceful gentleman and ferocious animalistic demon. As James Craig Holte argues:

> Through the work of the professionals at Hammer Films, the image of Dracula was transformed from the stylized black-and-white menace of Universal Pictures' Bela Legosi to the energetic terror Christopher Lee. Hammer created a vampire to suit the times. (1997: 65)

Hammer's Dracula was a Count for the youth market with energy to match. However, unlike Legosi's figure, he does not invade England (for budgetary reasons). Instead, he lives in a Germanic-sounding locale, where in *Dracula* and *Dracula, Prince of Darkness*, the English travel to visit him. Particularly in *Prince of Darkness*, it is the English that disturb the peace and cause the evil Other to rise again. While in *Dracula*, the Count rarely speaks, in *Prince of Darkness* he does not utter a single word; thus his animalistic, primal side is emphasised to an even greater extent. While he may look like a gentleman here, he certainly does not act like one. As the series progresses Dracula becomes more mechanical, barking one or two word orders at his servants, with his pronounced red-eyed stare and stature dominating the screen. *Prince of Darkness* expresses a transition from the gentlemanly, sophisticated Count to the animalistic, devil-like one.

Christopher Lee reveals his wild side in Dracula: Prince of Darkness

Vampirism has generally been associated with the hidden, symbolising an exhibition or excess of society's repressed behaviours and warning about their dangers. The vampire is the ultimate metaphor for the Other, and Dracula is considered the 'King of the Vampires'. Indeed, Otherness has been a major focus in most writing about vampire films. Psychoanalytical theory frames this in relation to sexuality and gender. Milly Williamson (2005) claims that Dracula has been read in the context of the Oedipus Complex, the Count serving as a symbol of sexual repression – he must kill the father (van Helsing) and his love for his mother drives him to have lustful relationships with several brides (Hammer's *The Brides of Dracula* plays on this concept by having the young Baron Meinster turn his mother first). However, Williamson criticises such approaches for ignoring femininity. She highlights the fear of active female sexuality prominent in the Dracula narrative (2005: 11), building on the work of Creed (1993).

Creed offers a psychoanalytical reading of the female vampire suggesting that it is 'monstrous – and also attractive – precisely because she does threaten to undermine the formal and highly symbolic relations of men and women essential to the continuation of patriarchal society' (1993: 61). Considering the myth of the 'vagina dentata', Creed argues against assumptions that the female vampire fangs are phallic, instead claiming that they are symbolic castrating genitals threatening patriarchal power. One could apply such a reading to *Prince of Darkness* and it would suggest that Helen and Diana are somewhat submissive in the opening of the film – though Helen is argumentative and tries to warn the men away from the castle, she is simply ignored. However, once she is turned, Helen presents a threat to the established patriarchal order. Thus, with her hair now free-flowing, wearing a long, white and revealing gown she thrusts herself towards Charles. Dracula hisses to tame her, while Charles and Father Sandor have no choice but to stake her. This monstrous-feminine must be destroyed if order is to be restored.

However, as Williamson also points out:

> Far from the vampire frightening us into rejecting its difference (and thus all the differences that it symbolises), the vampire has become an image of emulation, a glamorous outsider, a figure whose otherness we find versions of (sometimes ambivalently) in ourselves [...] the vampire offers a way of inhabiting difference with pride, for embracing defiantly an identity that the world at large sees as 'other'. (2005: 1)

Williamson speaks specifically here about contemporary portrayals of the vampire, and Hammer's films can be seen as fundamental in establishing this shift towards a vampire that audiences admire as well as fear. There is an irresistible lure about vampirism in *Prince of Darkness* first exhibited in Helen's transformation. This uptight, frustrated Victorian housewife seems to be liberated by the Count's bite as she literally lets her hair down and her cleavage bursts through her new attire. To some extent she is sexually liberated. While the men on-screen feel the need to tame and destroy her, her newfound liberation is more appealing to the spectator.

Furthermore as Hutchings contests, there are problems with the psychoanalytical approach, namely that 'the privileging of the sexual over issues to do with racial and class difference arguably neglects key elements in the *Dracula* story – namely the vampire's foreignness and his aristocracy' (2003: 16). As Hutchings posits, Stoker's Dracula is 'an amorphous figure, the threat he presents can one moment be intensely erotic, and at another moment be primarily racial, the threat of the foreigner to English national identity' (2003: 13). Such themes are pronounced in *Prince of Darkness*. Thus to consider Dracula's difference only on psychoanalytical terms is somewhat reductive.

As in most Hammer films, the doppelgänger is crucial to an understanding of *Prince of Darkness*'s presentation of Otherness. Thus, by examining how the film positions a group of stereotypical middle-class English people with Christian beliefs against the image of a ninetieth-century European Count, one can identify a specific uncertainty that the film raises about British identity – at a time (the mid-1960s) when class visibility, gender, sexuality and racial power were all undergoing major shifts. Viewed through the prism of the doppelgänger, Dracula's Otherness comes to represent a crisis in contemporary British values. A closer look at specific elements of the film evidences this clearly.

While the Dracula myth originates from Transylvania, this site is not mentioned in any of Hammer's European-based films. Place names such as 'Carlsbad' and 'Kleinberg' have a distinctly Germanic feel, as does much of the set and costume design. Hutchings warns of reading too much into the shift in location. He adds 'the space of the film is [...] an imaginative fantasy space, one that is not fully bound by notions of the real' (2003: 61-62). With Fisher's preference for the fairy tale rather than horror label, it is perhaps no surprise that the tale was transformed from its Gothic origins to the culture which bore the Brothers Grimm – whose 'grim' fairy tales the director often notes as an influence (in Ringel, 1975: 22).

Yet, the film does seem to point to specific real issues. *Prince of Darkness* is set ten years after the original Hammer film, in 1895 when the German Empire was well established with Wilhelm II as Emperor. Wilhelm was renowned for his aggressive attitude towards foreign policy, which is often, in part, blamed for the eventual start of World War I. Considering the significance of the doppelgänger, the Germanic contextualisation of Dracula can be seen as a mirror to the British Empire, which was gradually reforming into the less authoritative Commonwealth. Like the old German Empire, it had once been at the centre of Enlightenment and colonialism, but was now beginning to collapse.

Through the setting, the film emanates the fear/guilt dichotomy expressed more explicitly in *The Stranglers of Bombay*. While audiences might be tempted to look back at the Empire with nostalgia, presented by the lure of Dracula's life style, the aristocrat is presented as evil. As soon as we are attracted to this old way of living, we are immediately fearful of the Count's power and thus feel guilty for attracting towards it. Our ambiguous relationship with Dracula can be read as symbolic of the British Empire – celebrated for its achievements, yet shaped by a shameful history of genocide, colonialisation and slavery. Thus the Germanic setting can be understood as a locale doppelgänger of the British Empire and is repeated in many Hammer horrors. As discussed in the analysis of *Stranglers*, Arata (1996) identifies the significance of colonialism in Victorian Gothic literature, particularly in the work of Stoker. While in Stoker's time it served as comment on the unrest within the Empire, by the release of Hammer's Dracula films, the symbolism illustrates the threat of nostalgia – it might have seemed nice to have such power, but with it came great evil. As discussed in Chapter Two, Hammer's horror films were released at a time of great attitudinal shifts – long-held colonial and establishment beliefs were being aggressively challenged.

The class divisions exhibited in *Stranglers* are also expressed in *Prince of Darkness*. Though less explicitly associated with ethnicity in the latter, national difference is still crucial to status. Helen looks down on the locals in the tavern and the English men refuse to listen to the knowledgeable Sandor, assuming, with colonialist ignorance, that they know this foreign land better than its natives. The manner in which the travellers treat the locals is exaggerated in their doppelgänger Dracula, who forces those subservient to him, such as, Helen, Clove and Ludwig, to be hypnotically faithful. While this horrifies the tourists, it is an extreme amplification of the manner they expect those they consider lowly to act towards them.

A particularly interesting parallel in the film is the resurrection of the Count and the staking of Helen. Both are depicted as ritualistic, however Klove's movements are slow and he performs his bloody ceremony with respect and awe for his master. The visual presentation of this scene, while gruesome, is aesthetically pleasing. However, the staking of Helen is shocking. Father Sandor and the monks hold her down as she wriggles on the table. We cut between images of the monks manhandling Helen, her groaning and screaming face (in fact she screams before she is staked), and her chest (both a suggestion of how she will die and a titillating image). The repeated cutting between these shots establishes this sequence as particularly violent and Gregory Waller equates it with gang-rape (2010: 125). When Dracula attacks his victims, in contrast, there is a sexual tension, but one in which the victim is lured towards his irresistible hypnotic charm. In turning them, he gives them eternal life. The film's most shocking violent act, conversely, is orchestrated by humans, the dominating force of a group of 'virtuous' men on a frail female (albeit vampiric) body, and paved the way for rape fantasy sequences which later angered the censors such as *Straw Dogs, I Spit on Your Grave* (Dir. Meir Zarchi, 1978) and *Last House on the Left* (Dir.

Wes Craven, 1972). One can't help but feel Dracula gives his victims more dignity in death than the monks – and indeed the BBFC, who cut a gruesome depiction of Alan's body during the resurrection ritual while retaining the rape-like demise of Lucy.

References

Anon. 'Nietszche's idea of an overman and life from his point of view' https://ccrma.stanford.edu/~pj97/Nietzsche.htm [accessed on: 09/11/2014].

Arata, S.D. (1996). 'The Occidental Tourist: Dracula and the Anxiety of Reverse Colonization', in Grant, B.K. (ed.). *The Dread of Difference: Gender and the Horror Film*. Austin: University of Texas Press, pp161-171.

Creed, B. (1993). *The Monstrous- Feminine: Film, Feminism, Psychoanalysis*. London & New York: Routledge.

The Daily Cinema 'The Stranglers of Bombay' review. n8236, p5.

- 'Dracula, Prince of Darkness' review. n9159, p8.

Dudley, K. (2002). Hammer Goes East: The Stranglers of Bombay, in *Dark Terrors* 18th May, pp42-44.

Hallenbeck, B. G. (2010). *British Cult Cinema: The Hammer Vampire*. Bristol: Hemlock Books.

Hearn, M. & Barnes, A. (2007). *The Hammer Story: The Authorised History of Hammer*. London: Titan Books.

Hearn, M. (2009). *Hammer Glamour*. London: Titan Books.

Holte, J.C. (1997). *Dracula in the Dark: The Dracula Film Adaptations*. Westport & London: Greenwood Press.

Hunter, I.Q. (2013). *British Trash Cinema*. London: Palgrave Macmillan.

Hutchings, P. (2001). *Terence Fisher*. Manchester & New York: Manchester University Press.

- (2003) *Dracula*. London: I.B. Tauris.

Izhar, D. (2011). '*The Stranglers of Bombay* (1960) – Screenplay and Review Analysis', in '*Quiet India*': The Image of the Indian Patriot on Commercial

British Film and Television, 1956-1985. Newcastle-Upon-Tyne: Cambridge Scholars Publishing, pp112-128.

Kinsley, W. (1997). 'The Stranglers of Bombay', in *The House That Hammer Built* n2, pp110-112.

- (2008). *Hammer Films: The Bray Studios Years*. Richmond: Reynolds & Hearn Ltd.

Monthly Film Bulletin 'The Stranglers of Bombay' review. v27 n312, p10.

- 'The Gorgon' review. v.31 n369, p149.

Nietzsche, F. (2000). *The Basic Writings of Nietzsche*. Kaufmann, W. (TRANS), New York: The Modern Library.

Pirie, D. (2008). *A New Heritage of Horror*. London & New York: I.B. Tauris.

Waller, G. (2010). *The Living and the Undead: Slaying Vampires, Exterminating Zombies*. Illinois: The University of Illinois Press.

Wells, P. (2000). *The Horror Genre: From Beelzebub to Blair Witch*. London: Wallflower Press.

Williamson, M. (2005). *The Lure of the Vampire: Gender, Fiction and Fandom from Bram Stoker to Buffy*. London & New York: Wallflower Press.

Variety (1959). 'The Stranglers of Bombay' review. 23rd December, p17.

- (1964). 'The Gorgon' review. 26th August, p6.

CHAPTER 7: THE FALL OF HAMMER

Alfred Hitchcock's *Psycho* set a new precedent for horror that would eventually pose a serious threat to Hammer. It was set in modern times and featured a human killer. While a spate of companies created Hammer imitations, such as Tigon's *Witchfinder General* and Erica Productions Inc.'s *Count Yorga, Vampire*, olde-world, fantasy horror was gradually to be replaced by a gritty, modern variation, with films such as *Repulsion* (Dir. Roman Polanski, 1965), *Night of the Living Dead*, *Rosemary's Baby* and *Last House on the Left*. Hammer's desperation was clear in the tagline for their last 1970s horror film, *To the Devil a Daughter*, which read:

> The evil power of black magic has fascinated millions of cinema-goers. First... 'Rosemary's Baby'. Then ... 'The Exorcist'. And now a motion picture that probes further into the mysteries of the occult than any has dared before!

Hammer tried several strategies to compete with the emerging modern horror style, but sadly failed as they gradually lost American backing. These techniques can be seen in *The Devil Rides Out*, which gives horror a human face with an occult setting in the 1920s; *Dracula A.D. 1972* set in contemporary London and Hammer's first (and only) film to focus on a group of modern teenagers; and finally *The Legend of the 7 Golden Vampires*, a transnational production which hybridises the then-popular kung fu craze with classic Hammer horror.

The Devil Rides Out

Director Terence Fisher
Year of Release 1968 Running Time 95 minutes Certificate X

> I really must congratulate you, I think this is probably the best Hammer picture I have ever seen and think that it should be a great commercial success. (John Trevelyan, Secretary of the BBFC, in a memo to James Carreras dated 23 April 1968)

Synopsis: *Rural England 1929, Duc de Richleau and Rex van Ryn are concerned they haven't see their friend Simon for months. They visit his manor, only to discover he is hosting a party with his 'astronomical* society' which has a strict rule about thirteen members. De Richleau, convinced Simon is lying, searches the house and discovers a room set-up for satanic rituals. It is clear the astronomical society is a cover for a cult led by Mocata. De Richleau takes Simon back to his house, attempting to free him from Mocata's hold, but it is too strong and he is compelled to escape. Simon and another young protégée Tanith attend a Black Mass in the woods, preparing for their satanic baptism. Rex and De Richleau sabotage the ceremony and rescue Simon and Tanith. De Richleau takes them to his friends, the Eaton's home, but in doing so places the family in danger. Inside the house, he creates a protective circle to repel evil which presents itself in many forms including a giant tarantula, the Angel of Death, and the figure of Peggy, the Eaton's youngest daughter. Peggy is snatched for a sacrificial ceremony by the Satanists. Tanith is killed. As De Richleau, Rex and the Eatons discover the ritual, Marie Eaton is possessed and stops the devil-worshippers. Time is reversed and Tanith returns to Simon, De Richleau and the others.

The Devil Rides Out should have hailed exciting times for Hammer, but retrospectively it can now be seen as the beginning of the studio's demise. It was released the year Hammer won the Queen's Award for Industry, and the film, based on a Dennis Wheatley novel, is considered one of the studio's best. It was directed by Terence Fisher and starred Christopher Lee, yet shifts from Victorian-set monster horror (though as some of the earlier films like The Gorgon are post-Victorian, it is a somewhat arbitrary differentiation) to twentieth-century devil worshipping. Hammer took advantage of the BBFC's new leniency regarding occult subject matter and it was much praised by BBFC Secretary John Trevelyan. Unfortunately, however, it was released the same year as Rosemary's Baby, The Night of the Living Dead and The Witchfinder General. While the latter, produced by Tigon, was highly influenced by Hammer's style, as Sinclair McKay (2007) suggests it differs in two distinct ways: firstly it removes the sense of distance Hammer's costume-base fantasy worlds had created, by invading these spaces with contemporary moving camerawork; and secondly it portrays virtue 'as the victim throughout', thus is much darker than Hammer's film, offering 'the very opposite of escapism' (2007: 124).

In America, Roman Polanski and George A. Romero were tapping into contemporary anxieties at a time when people were losing faith in their government and the war effort in Vietnam, a conflict that affected

Hammer's fortunes directly. As McKay notes, 'the US Government did not want to see funds going overseas' (2007: 129). Thus, along with the changing face of Hollywood's corporations as many of the major studio heads of the classical period retired, 'cutbacks were the new orders of the day' (2007: 130). While Hammer still managed to retain a relationship with Warner Bros., it was no longer as easy to secure deals. Ironically just as the occult and devil worshipping became major topics in American horror films (though one must remember that much of the country's horror was produced outside of the major studios), Warners disliked the topic and preferred that Hammer return to their classic monsters. As Hammer was attempting to update their style for a new youth generation, it was being held back by its dependence on American backing.

The Devil Rides Out seems to pre-empt the shift that would happen during the next decade of international horror production, yet it retains much of the Hammer period charm. It offers an update of the Hammer style, particularly emphasised by the foregrounding of the occult, setting the film in the twentieth century and experimenting more obviously with special effects. Unlike earlier Hammer films, *The Devil Rides Out* transposes the studio's Victorian Gothic to 1920s England. No longer is there an implied paralleling between a foreign, historical land and contemporary Britain, the horror is firmly rooted in a world audiences recognise (if not from their own lives, then at least from photographs or memories of their living relatives). However, the stately manor house, such an important trope of earlier Hammer films, still remains, its décor little changed. This is significant because it still roots evil in a Gothic past – the house has clearly been passed down through the centuries, as have the occultist symbols. While guests at Simon's party wear fashionable 1920s outfits rather than Victorian attire, the message about his companions is the same as for the likes of Frankenstein, Dracula or Hyde – the bourgeoisie are dangerous.

Particularly interesting is the way Fisher situates symbols of contemporary culture within the Gothic context. When Rex rescues Tanith, they hurriedly drive to de Richleau's house for protection. In the car, Hammer's common leitmotif, the mirror (here, in the form of the rear-view mirror) reveals the duality in her character. The mirror often appears in Hammer films to explicate the liminality between good and evil. In *The Two Faces of Dr Jekyll*, Henry looks into the mirror and sees his darker side, Edward Hyde (a motif repeated in *Dr Jekyll and Sister Hyde* [Dir. Seth Holt, 1971]). In *Countess Dracula*, Elizabeth is tormented by the reflection of her true, aged facade. In *The Devil Rides Out*, Tanith looks into the rear-view mirror and a close-up of her eyes is accompanied with the haunting voice of Mocata, signifying the satanic side of the young girl, a repressed part of her soul (suggested by her name), vulnerable to release by occultist ritual. *The Devil Rides Out* thus transposes Gothic tropes into a twentieth century context. Rather than a hanging mirror in a laboratory or a decorative vanity one in a decadent castle, here the potential dualism of the individual is revealed through the rear-view mirror of a 1920s automobile.

Mocata's possessive stare in The Devil Rides Out

The occult, like the Gothic, has a particularly rich history in English culture, from the pagan ancestry of the country to Elizabethan alchemy, Aleister Crowley and the writing of Shakespeare and Marlowe to Victorian organisations such as the Hermetic Order of the Golden Dawn Society and the work of novelists such as Wheatley (Fry 2008: 15; Ransome 2005: 36). During Hammer's reign over British horror, there were two periods of occult film production in the country. The first, 1957-1964, Leon Hunt considers a reaction against Hammer's visualisation of horror with a focus on the 'unseen' (2001: 82) and the second, 1966 until 1976, in which Hammer played a more active role. The occult context is clearly established in the opening credits of *The Devil Rides Out* in which Hammer's traditional wide shot of a middle-European castle is replaced with animated graphics of occultist symbols, most recognisably the symbol of Baphomet – the Sabbatic Goat in an inverted pentagram and an interesting repetition of the figure crossed-legged holding two fingers up, not dissimilar from the peace-sign of counter-culture.

Ransome posits four particular tropes of the occult film: the will to power, hidden locations such as woodlands to carry out ceremonies (outside of mainstream society), the anti-church organisation as encouraging one to be flawed or overtly sexualised, and the Crowley figure: 'the Magus or Witch, a character who gains other-worldly powers through invocation, ritual and sacrifice' (2005: 36-37). Furthermore, he suggests the rescue narrative is common to the sub-genre. *The Devil Rides Out* clearly illustrates these conventions. Mocata represents the Crowley-like figurehead of the Satanist group. As Hunt argues, fictionalised images of Crowley tend to be 'uncanny and magnetic, hysterically phallic, queer in the broadest sense of the term' (2001: 87). Mocata's dominating stare (often shown in close-up, like Dracula's blood-shot eyes) and his power over men and women, establish him as the bisexual Crowley-like figure (2001: 87-8). During the baptism sequence, Mocata watches over his disciples, his robe a vibrant purple clearly distinguishable from their plain white clothes. As he sees them cavorting, he smiles with pleasure. Throughout the film he bewitches others with his Dracula-like stare.

The will to power is most interestingly tackled in the final ritual when Mocata's sacrifice is interrupted by Marie, who seems to have been possessed by a higher being. While it would be simple to assume it is the voice of God, she states, 'only those who love without desire will have power granted to them in the darkest hour' which seems to echo the hedonistic qualities of Satanism. The Satanic statement (taken from the contemporary Satanic Bible) 'Satan represents kindness to those who deserve it instead of love wasted on ingrates' (Anton LaVey, 1969: 13) is not dissimilar from Marie's proclamation. For LaVey, the leader of the modern Church of Satan, the Dark Lord might celebrate indulgence and emotional gratification, but he is not without some moral framework, believing those who are evil should be punished. In this moment then, it is ambiguous whether Marie speaks the words of God or the Devil himself – revealing potentially the true beliefs of the Antichrist, rather than the barbarism promoted by Mocata who advertises himself as all-powerful. Mocata does not try to fight this being; rather, he and the disciples move out of Marie's way as if she is a power to be respected.

Kinsley claims that Christopher Lee went to the British Museum 'to find a genuine black magic incarnation to use for the Sussamma Ritual... different in Matheson's final screenplay' (Kinsley 1997: 329). It is not

Christian; rather, magick is fought with magick. After the ceremony, Mocata's soul is taken by the Angel of Death, and though De Richleau suggests 'He [God] is the one we must thank', it is rather ambiguous and his final exchange with Simon suggests their potential naivety and reaffirms that there is a lot 'hidden' (occult) to man. The ceremonies, held in back rooms of large manor houses or woodlands, express the secrecy of the organisation and its practices, though it is interesting that Simon's house, albeit in a sparsely populated rural area, suggests that the higher echelons of mainstream English society has spaces designed for such events hinting that they are more embedded in the quotidian than spectators may think. Thus evil here is not the Devil, but the man who wishes to possess ultimate power equivalent to Satan.

Pirie claims that 'until this point Hammer had had little success with witchcraft and black magic' (2008: 74). He highlights *The Witches*, a failure, as Hammer's only other foray into this arena. However, the occult is a theme which runs through many of the studio's early works and *The Devil Rides Out* merely modernises and emphasises this particular convention. For example, *The Stranglers of Bombay* and *The Plague of Zombies* both open with occultist ceremonies where sacrifices are made to ancient or foreign Gods (or Goddess in the case of the former). *The Reptile* implies an occultist back-story which has led to Anna's misfortune. In *Dracula, Prince of Darkness*, Klove performs an elaborate ritual to resurrect his master. In all of these films, however, the occult is placed in a foreign context – it represents the threat of a barbaric other culture, which also serves as an interesting critical mirror for the actions of the British characters. While Hunt argues that 1966-68 marked a definitive shift from Judaeo-Christian dualism in British horror to an interest in pagan roots (2001: 84), other belief systems are portrayed in many earlier Hammer films. However, *The Devil Rides Out* is distinguishable from its predecessors because it situates occultist behaviour deep in the heart of England, seemingly the Home Counties. Paul has not been tainted by the influence of an exotic people, but rather by well-to-do aristocratic English men and women who are rather fussy about the exclusivity of their gatherings. Interestingly, the original novel has the heroes travel to American to kill Mocata, but screenwriter Richard Matheson retained the entire narrative in England (Dudley, 1992: 5).

Ransome offers a useful definition of the occult:

> Occult literally means 'hidden' so all Horror could be described
> as occult in the sense that all Horror deals with things that are
> suppressed, repressed, traditionally denied or habitually ignored. The
> Occult Horror sub-genre, however, specifically deals with the esoteric
> and magickal (as differentiated from the magic of Paul Daniels) that
> exists outside the exoteric realm of mainstream religion. (2005: 36)

While the occult is often related to non-mainstream belief systems, it
is particularly interesting that *The Devil Rides Out* seems to allude to
Christianity through its ritualistic mise-en-scène. Parallels between
Christianity and the occult are apparent in many of the later Hammer
films – the ritual to resurrect Count Dracula in *Dracula A.D. 1972* is held
in a church, while *Twins of Evil* positions puritans, who never hesitate to
burn promiscuous young women for witchcraft, against a vampire. As
Simon enters the closing ritual of *The Devil Rides Out* he looks down to
see Mocata situated at an alter, standing higher than his disciples, the
occult leader is surrounded by candle sticks – both single candles on
golden stands as one might recognise from a church, and seven-stick
holders reminiscent of the Jewish menorah. Mocata establishes himself
as the priest-like figure, rubbing his hands together as if in prayer as he
proclaims the beginning of the ceremony. His assistants wear similar
purple robes to him, while the disciples wear white – a symbol of purity,
as one would expect a new convert to wear at a Christian baptism. The
disciplines fall to their knees in a praying position. The stark contrast to
modern Christianity of course, is the sacrifice to be performed. However
it reminds the spectator of the legacy of Christian brutality including the
burning of heretics and witches – the fear associated with the occult here,
then, might also be attributed to the history of organised Western religion.

Hunt suggests conflict between the new and old religions in the 1960 and
1970s occult films expresses issues about British identity:

> First, the growing popular interest in paganism was partly bound
> up with uncovering a more 'authentic' national identity and culture.
> [...] Second, the conflict between 'old' and 'new' faiths was a way of
> talking about the relationship between the upheavals of the late 1960s
> – the emergence of youth and 'counter' cultures, permissiveness, the
> possibility of revolution. (2001: 92-93)

The slippage between the occult or satanic and Christian rituals and spaces in *The Devil Rides Out* emphasises the blurry distinctions between the two cultures. While the growing interest in paganism and occultism was inspired by New Age culture, which may have been considered a threat in the eyes of devout Christians, it also highlighted the restraints of traditional, organised religion in conflict with a new, more liberated world. Thus, both cultures were neither necessarily right nor wrong; both existed alongside each other. It was an era of uncertainty regarding the sacred, not one of complete revolution or denial. New Age culture did not refute worship; it just replaced old systems. While New Age covers a wide range of belief systems, Carrol L. Fry notes their uniting factor was 'the assumption that the world is but one plane of reality and that other levels can be reached, usually through some practice definable as occult' (2008: 28-29).

In *The Devil Rides Out*, characters attempt to reach the Underworld and try to incorporate it into their lived-world through satanic rituals. Satanism is exemplary of the complex relationship between mainstream religions and the occult, for it cannot exist without Christianity. LaVey (1969) writes a re-evaluation of Christian beliefs in 'The Satanic Bible', rather than an entirely new faith. It is a reaction against organised, traditional religion, rather than something completely new, and in situating itself as a comparative (and ironically a somewhat organised) faith, similarities can naturally be drawn. *The Devil Rides Out* subtly critiques just how non-radical occultist behaviour might be, despite its desire for difference and rebellion, through subtly highlighting its parallels with Christianity. This comparison also reminds spectators of the barbaric history of Christianity by associating traditional ceremonial practices with the 'primitive' occult. Furthermore it highlights the potential for evil in man, for it is a transcendent being that saves the characters in the final sequence – one whose identity is somewhat ambiguous.

Hammer planned several Wheatley adaptations, including versions of his books *The Haunting of Toby Jugg* (1948), *Gateway to Hell* (1970) and *Strange Conflict* (1941), but *The Devil Rides Out*, while somewhat successful in the UK, was not well received in the United States and worried financers. The studio subsequently turned only two of his works into films, the novel *Uncharted Seas* (1938) became the sea-adventure *The Lost Continent* (Dir. Michael Carreras, 1968), while *To The Devil A Daughter* (from his 1953 novel of the same name) would be Hammer's final horror of the 1970s. After *The Devil Rides Out*, Warner Bros. recommended the studio returned to its old favourites: Frankenstein and Dracula.

Dracula A.D. 1972 (1972)

Director Alan Gibson
Year of Release 1972 Running Time 96 minutes Certificate X

> *Dracula A.D. 1972* gets more entertaining with the passing of time, and is perhaps best enjoyed as an endearing, if naive, picture of an era that never was. (Hearn & Barnes, 2007: 157)

Synopsis: *1872, van Helsing and Dracula both die in their final battle. A young man, who watches their fight, collects the Count's ashes.*

The film fast forwards to 1970s London. Young Jessica van Helsing (a distant relative of the vampire hunter) is encouraged by her grandfather to get involved in the family's occult research, but she is not interested. With friends, she heads to a gig in the now dilapidated St Bartolph's Church (where the original van Helsing is buried), but, unknown to her, the event is actually a Black Mass ritual. She is convinced their friend Johnny Alucard (take a moment to spell his name backwards) has killed their friend Laura.

One by one, Johnny sacrifices their friends to the now resurrected Count, who is ultimately after Jessica as revenge against van Helsing. However, Jessica's grandfather leads the vampire hunt and condemns Dracula to the grave by thrusting a spade through his chest as a makeshift stake. The Count turns to dust.

Hammer tried to refresh the Dracula series by situating the Count in modern day London. As we have seen, across the Atlantic, a new breed of American horror was developing and among the human killers, zombies and occult stories there would also be an attempt to refresh the vampire narrative, *Martin* (Dir. George A. Romero, 1976). *Dracula A.D. 1972* is generally considered the worst Hammer horror and exemplary of the studio's later years. While Hearn and Barnes look nostalgically upon the film in the above review, the *Monthly Film Bulletin*'s verdict that the film is 'abortive and totally unimaginative' is more representative of thoughts at the time (Freeman 2002: 198). By contrast, *Martin* was recently voted one of the top 100 horror films (the only Hammer film to feature is *Dracula*) (*Time Out*, 2014). To consider how Hammer's modernisation of the vampire myth failed, a comparison with *Martin* is useful.

Also set in the 1970s, *Martin* is the story of a teenage boy who travels to Pittsburgh to live with an aging relative and his granddaughter. His elderly cousin Cuda assumes Martin has the family's Nosferatu curse. However Martin tries to convince Cuda that there is no magic and that vampires are just costumes. But this doesn't stop Martin injecting victims with needles to put them asleep, before draining and drinking their blood. Discovering Martin has attacked in his neighbourhood, Cuda stakes the young 'vampire' through the heart.

While Martin lives in a recognisable contemporary American city, Hammer's resurrected Dracula does not move amongst the streets of modern-day London, relying instead on Johnny to source his victims. Despite the contemporary context, *Dracula A.D. 1972* retains Hammer's classical aesthetic for scenes involving ritual or the Count, and little attempt is made to integrate the character into modern society. As Hunter argues: 'Despite their formal experimentation [Hammer's] later vampire films still worked within the conservative moral framework of traditional Gothic' (2002: 139).

Hammer's desire to retain its classical style can be seen in the opening sequence, the 'final' battle between van Helsing and Dracula, which Cooper considers 'as good as anything in the series' (2016: 88). Close-ups build anticipation with cuts between the wheel, the ropes securing the horses breaking and reaction shots of Dracula's grimacing face, a tree and then part of the cart as it smashes into a tree. A lone man riding on a horse is then momentarily seen in a long shot, before the film returns to the showdown between van Helsing and the Count. The former discovers Dracula has been staked by the coach wheel and finishes him off by pushing it deeper before finally dying himself. Dracula's body dissolves to dust, an image Hammer fans will recognise from earlier films and the close-up of his signet ring references *Dracula*. A lone horseman then arrives to collect the Count's ashes. The tension built by the close-ups, the inclusion of Hammer's two most famous male stars and the period mise-en-scène establishes a classic Hammer aesthetic.

One of the distinctions from earlier Hammer films, however, is the funk-style soundtrack, which acts as a motif throughout the film, and has disappointed many critics. As Pirie suggests it 'must rank among the worse Hammer ever commissioned' (2008: 111). *Martin* has a similar soundtrack, which in that instance adds verisimilitude, highlighting the ambiguity about whether the protagonist is a supernatural creature or a more mundane serial killer. *Martin*'s soundtrack and mise-en-scène creates realism, while in *Dracula A.D. 1972* the contrast between Hammer's traditional Grand Guignol aesthetic when Dracula is on screen with the sub-Jazz funk score is deeply incongruous, particularly when van Helsing hunts for the Count in a sequence which resembles a 1970s police procedural rather than Hammer Gothic.

Despite the contemporary context, the film retains Count Dracula's classic Hammer iconography, which Martin mocks as nothing more than a 'costume'. While Hammer's early films are ambiguous portrayals of good and evil, and colonial culture, *Dracula A.D. 1972* clearly establishes the Count as foreign to the time and place. In contrast, as Linnie Blake contests: 'Romero seems to argue that Martin is an example of the pernicious effects that mass culture has on the subjectivity of the American individual; the individual who, like Martin himself, seems destined to suffer from a kind of nationally-specific schizophrenia' (2002: 159). Martin, unlike Dracula then, represents an inherent danger in contemporary disaffected American society, rather than an external threat.

The church where Johnny holds the ritual is traditionally Gothic. It has long, thin windows, pale brown walls and is covered in weeds, suggesting its neglect – it belongs to the old world and the old horror. As Johnny speaks, he is surrounded by fog and moody blue lighting. He wears a brown robe and holds a silver chalice at the altar decorated by candles. Despite the supposed 1972 setting, this sequence would not look out of place in any of the period Hammer films. As Johnny celebrates the fact he has summoned the Count, Dracula intones, 'It was my will' and lifts his hand to be kissed in an awkward gesture that suggests he might be suffering rigor mortis. This mechanical motion is typical of his actions throughout the film, and while Lee's Dracula is still a threatening presence, the actor was openly disdainful of the project.

Hammer's classic period aesthetic remains, despite Dracula A.D. 1972 *moving into the modern era*

Hinds protests that the monster is always the hero of Hammer's horror films (in Klemensen, 1976: 17). However in *Dracula A.D. 1972*, the Count can be considered the protagonist only by virtue of the title as he has even less screen time than in the earlier films. In contrast, Martin is clearly the protagonist in Romero's film. The spectator is invited to follow his story and to empathise with the killer because all his victims are flat characters who are not developed. He is even heard in voiceover as he confesses to a radio presenter. Furthermore, Martin mimics Dracula's appearance, wearing the same cloak with a pale face and over-exaggerated fangs (clearly purchased from a fancy dress store) in order to scare Cuda. As his cousin falls in terror, Martin laughs and exclaims 'it's only a costume' repeatedly. Martin doesn't react to the priest, garlic or a cross, but is eventually killed by the stake (though his body remains a human corpse). He repeatedly explains that there is no such thing as real magic – particularly when he shows his cousin's grand-daughter a finger slicer with a real and phony blade. Throughout the film, black-and-white sequences place Martin in a Universal-style horror film and one of the most interesting cross-cut sequences comes at the film's finale when a modern-day Martin on the run from the police is juxtaposed against a black-and-white Gothic version of the villain chased at night by a torch-wielding crowd. *Martin* is a transitional film drawing parallels between the old and the new horror, while *Dracula A.D. 1972* fails to reconcile old Hammer with new interpretations of the genre.

While Martin can be read as a figure who represents many contemporary American anxieties, Pirie argues convincingly that Hammer 'did not even attempt to come to terms with the opening problem of any modern Dracula: namely how to relate the vampire figure to contemporary society'

(2008: 110). Furthermore, he considers that Bram Stoker achieved this in the original novel, bringing an ancient vampire into the Victorian era by creating a Count who could 'deal with legal matters, railway timetables and other aspects of the Victorian world. This made him more, not less, frightening. And it enabled his readers to imagine the Count's subtle infiltration of London society' (ibid.), whereas *Dracula A.D. 1972*'s Count is confined to the dilapidated church.

In the next film in the series, *The Satanic Rites of Dracula* (Dir. Alan Gibson, 1973), the Count plays a more active role in modern society, blackmailing scientists and acting as a manipulative property developer. However, in shifting completely to the 1970s world, it abandons the typical Hammer charm. After these two films, Christopher Lee would refuse to return as the Count for Hammer, but the studio would make one more Dracula story.

The Legend of the 7 Golden Vampires

Director Roy Ward Baker and Cheh Chang (martial arts)
Year of Release 1974 Running Time 83 minutes Certificate X

> I'm tempted to suggest that Hammer and Shaw were simply slightly ahead of their times, as the un-stoppable tide of Eastern fantasy pouring out from the studios of Hong Kong testifies there is now a huge market for this sort of thing. (*Flesh and Blood*, 1984: 49)

Synopsis: *Kah, a Buddhist monk travels through Transylvania to Castle Dracula. He summons the Count to tell him that the Seven Golden Vampires' power is fading. Dracula offers to help on the provision that he possesses Kah's body.*

1904, China: Professor Lawrence van Helsing gives an unsuccessful lecture about the Chinese vampire legend. Hsi Ching informs him that he knows the legend is true because his grandfather battled the vampires. He seeks the Professor's help, with his brothers and sister, to return to their birth village and destroy the six remaining vampires. They are joined by an adventurous young Western female Vanessa Buren and van Helsing's son Leyland.

Battling through several encounters with the vampires, Ching's sister is captured and taken to their sacrificial altar. Leyland attempts to save her, but a vampire tries to drain his blood. After much battling in spectacular kung fu fights, the Golden Vampires are slain. As the survivors leave the temple, but van Helsing encounters Kah. Dracula reveals himself and attacks, but van Helsing stabs him through the heart with a spear and he disintegrates to dust. Hammer's Dracula is finally dead.

The Legend of the 7 Golden Vampires was Hammer's penultimate 1970s horror film. The studio was losing American backing, therefore sought alternative funding from the rising Hong Kong industry. Hammer struck a deal with the Shaw Brothers, one of the world's most successful film production companies, to create a kung fu vampire film. While such hybridisation was certainly unusual at the time, as the above Flesh and Blood review implies, the film was a forerunner of a successful 1980s Hong Kong genre. Unfortunately by the time spiritual/horror kung fu films such as Encounters of a Spooky Kind (Dir. Sammo Kam-Bo Hung, 1980), A Chinese Ghost Story (Dir. Siu-Tung Ching, 1987), We are Going to Eat You (Dir. Hark Tsui, 1980) and Mr Vampire (Dir. Ricky Lau, 1985) became popular with cult audiences, Hammer and Shaw Brothers were both defunct. The 1980s films combine kung fu and horror in a tongue-in-cheek way, typical of eighties youth cinema. In contrast, The Legend of the 7 Golden Vampires continues Hammer's traditional straight-acting style and was not quite as successful (though it has become something of a cult classic today). While popular elsewhere, its American release was delayed and it was severely cut before being released in a butchered version called The 7 Brothers meet Dracula.

Criticism of the film tends to focus on the cultural clash of Hammer and kung fu. For example, Films Illustrated stated, 'East is East and West is West and ne'er the twain shall meet, quoth the saga. Certainly this hybrid is less than the sum of its parts' (in Rigby 2001: 54); while Derek Elley claims, 'one wishes the film had either been written and directed by the Chinese themselves or left to Hammer without the presence of Hong Kong stars' (1975: 43). Verina Glaessner (1975) accuses the film of misunderstanding the role of hand-to-hand combat in Chinese cinema and David McGillivray states 'it is much more talkative than the average Chinese spectacle, while the horror is stubbornly non-horrific' (1974: 15).

Few critics seem to appreciate the negotiation and compromise necessary for generic and cultural hybridisation. *The Legend of the 7 Golden Vampires* must be understood as a film which not only blends two disparate genres, but also two distinct cultures. Notable areas where these cultures differ include: their interpretation of the vampire myth, the representation of women and their philosophical underpinnings. However, the theatrical roots of kung fu performance certainly had the potential to integrate with Hammer's Grand Guignol style, and visually the film is one of the studio's most spectacular. The film points to cultural differences in several scenes.

Kung fu has its roots in Chinese opera, a particularly colourful, performance style featuring 'extravagant costumes, bright full-face make-up, Olympic-class gymnastics, and both weapon and empty-handed combat' (Ben Logan, 1995: 9), and *wu xia pian* (early films based on *wu xia* literature, literally meaning 'chivalrous combat film' (Sek Kei, 1994: 27)). These stories combine the 'wu' (martial arts) and 'xia' (valiant knight), who could be a man or a woman (Rance, 2005: 23). Such stories are often rooted in the supernatural and foreground themes of vengeance influenced by Confucian philosophy rather than the Christian dualism, or Nietzschean ambiguity one might associate with Hammer. In contrast to sword fighting, the early hand-combat kung fu films that evolved from *wu xia pain* featured lower class individuals on a quest avenging the murder of their family. *The Legend of the 7 Golden Vampires* follows this tradition with Ching's story. Van Helsing is cautious about the trip, but the brothers plead with him to join them. Despite their lowly status, the kung fu hero always finds great courage, which enables them to destroy evil. Ching is positioned in opposition to a wealthy man who propositions Vanessa early in the film. When the man has her and Leyland attacked, Ching and his brothers come to the rescue. Furthermore, Ching's sister, though she is captured by the vampires and needs to be saved by the white male hero (more traditionally a Western plot device), is as powerful and skilled at martial arts as her brothers. Hammer seems to have attempted to mirror her with the free-spirited Vanessa – though somewhat sexualised (but not as much as most of Hammer's later women characters), she is financially independent and craves adventure.

Furthermore, the Chinese vampire is not a sophisticated, mysterious and suave gentleman; he is closer to the Western concept of the zombie.

Logan identifies the major distinctions of the Chinese vampire:

> These reanimated corpses hop across the Mainland countryside,
> held in check by a painted incarnation pinned to their forehead. If the
> incarnation is removed, it's like pulling the stake from Dracula's heart.
> A blood-sucking ghoul is once again free to stalk the land [...] Another
> major difference is that Chinese people really believe these creatures
> existed, while hardly anyone in the West believes in Dracula [...] the
> methods used by the Chinese movie ghostbusters to dispel evil are still
> employed in certain regions of China. Rather than being pure flights of
> fancy, Hong Kong horror films reflect the genuine beliefs and fears of a
> superstitious people. (1995: 101)

The film's opening establishes the unification of the two cultures. Dracula
is transposed back to his literary origins in Transylvania, presumably for
the benefit of Chinese audiences (who would be more familiar with the
novel than with Hammerland). Kah's golden yellow robe and long black
hair and beard establish him as a Buddhist monk. He steadily works
his way through the countryside; close-ups of his staff accompanied by
wide shots of his wavering body illustrate the struggle. Images of the
deserted countryside and a lone traveller on a quest are typical of Chinese
action cinema. As a monk he highlights the spiritual origins of kung fu
(the Shaolin monastery to which many of the genre's films pay homage).
However, there is soon a close-up of a large Christian cross from which
the camera tilts down – its presence looms over the space. Upon entering
the castle, Kah's small, frail shape is over-powered by the Gothic interior.
As he bows before Dracula's grave in wide shot, the two cultures merge.
This is further emphasised by the vampiric transformation, as Dracula
consumes Kah's physical shape. The two face each other in close-up,
their appearances starkly different. Dracula even notes Kah's 'ghastly
image'. Smoke emerges from the bottom of the frame, as the two turn
in a full circle, Dracula with his arms firmly on Kah's shoulders. Kah's
cries get weaker as the Count pushes him down. Dracula has his back
completely to the camera and then as he lifts his arms, an edit transforms
him into Kah, who turns to reveal himself to the camera and speaks the
voice of the Count, firmly uniting Western and Eastern mythology.

A Chinese vampire rises from the ground in The Legend of the 7 Golden Vampires

The appearance and death of the vampires in this film is perhaps the most gruesome in Hammer's history. Such a grotesque style has been repeated since in horrors such as *Evil Dead: Army of Darkness* (Dir. Sam Raimi, 1992 – interestingly, Raimi suggests he was deeply influenced by Hong Kong cinema (Logan, 1995: 108)). The images juxtapose Hammer's Grand Guignol with the exaggerated, colour-saturated style of Chinese opera, and amalgamate these two aesthetics with the Western and Eastern mythos of the vampire. As van Helsing tells his students about the legend, it plays out as flashback. The Golden Vampires are first seen during this sequence, wearing golden masks to cover their eyes, exposing decrepit, decaying grey flesh on the bottom of their faces. Their movements are awkward and zombie-like. Only Kah possesses normal bodily functions. As he sounds a gong, an undead hand rises in close-up from the ground, followed by several shots of masked figures pushing through the earth. A green mist covers the screen, as one of the undead surveys the area with only the top of his body protruding from the ground. In slow motion, figures begin to accumulate, the wind turns into screams and harsh squealing noises. The creatures are more ghoul-like than Hammer's refined vampires.

Perhaps where the film deviates most from traditional Hammer horror is in its philosophical roots. Ching is a man of virtue who must defend his family's honour, while Kah is tainted by his involvement with the Golden Vampires and finds the pure evil he seeks in the form of Dracula. The two men are clearly defined as binary opposites. In contrast, the majority of Hammer's male leads are ambiguous, and seeking the will to power often kills them (e.g. Frankenstein and Henry Jekyll). Other Hammer leads express ambiguity through their battle between knowledge and the good life, and the will to power as discussed in the previous chapter. However, clear distinctions between good and evil in *The Legend of the 7 Golden Vampires* distinguishes it from classic Hammer films, which the Shaw Brothers believed to be essential for foreign audiences (Teo, 2005: 195).

Retrospectively writing about the film's production reveals that the cultural clashes appear to be more behind the scenes than on screen, the most jarring element being the difference between the dialogue scenes shot in a typically restrained Hammer style and the action sequences. Geoff Mayer notes that Run Run Shaw wanted the latter to be shot by a local director, while Baker tried to insist that consistency be retained. Eventually Shaw got his way with Chang Cheh shooting the kung fu scenes, but this led to the film having two distinct styles as Baker had feared (2004: 59). Baker was never satisfied with the outcome, but implicit in his reaction to what he perceived as the 'primitive' set-up in Hong Kong is a reluctance to embrace the local style. Similarly, the Shaw Brothers' over-emphasis on a simplistic binary good versus evil and demand for the Dracula prologue and epilogue in order to market the film using the Dracula brand didn't help tension either. There seemed to be a misunderstanding by both sides of the other's culture.

If considered in the context of the mid-century 'cinema of attractions' as suggested in Chapter Three, the cult status that *The Legend of the 7 Golden Vampires* currently enjoys can be understood in terms of the spectacle it offers. It is a film about watching: the martial arts experts move in seemingly magical ways (though regrettably this is underplayed in the film) and grotesque transformations of human flesh are performed with special effects. It is a film about the pleasure (or disgust) of film viewing, but, as the review from *Flesh and Blood* explains, as one of the first films to combine vampires and kung fu, it was ahead of its time and the box office reflected this. Hammer released only one more horror film, *To the Devil a Daughter*, in the 1970s, and soon after the studio would enter hibernation as a film production company until the twenty-first century.

References

Blake, L. (2002). 'Another One for the Fire: George A. Romero's American Theology of the Flesh', in Mendik, Xavier (ed.). *Necronomicon Presents: Shocking Cinema of the Seventies*. Hereford: Noir Publishing, pp 151-165.

Cooper, I. (2016). *Frightmares: A History of British Horror Cinema*. Leighton Buzzard: Auteur.

Dudley, K. (1992). 'Dennis Wheatley & Hammer's Film Adaptations', in *Dark Terror* n1, pp5-10.

Elley, D. (1975). 'The Legend of the 7 Golden Vampires', in *Films and Filming* v21 n1, p43.

Flesh and Blood (1994). 'The Legend of the 7 Golden Vampires'. n3, p49.

Freeman, N. (2002). 'London Kills Me: The English Metropolis in British Horror Films of the 1970s', in Mendik, X. (ed). *Necronomicon Presents: Shocking Cinema of the Seventies*. Hereford: Noir Publishing, pp193-209.

Fry, C. L. (2008). *Cinema of the Occult: New Age, Satanism, Wicca and Spiritualism in Film*. Bethlehem: Lehigh University Press.

Glaessner, V. (1974). *Kung Fu: Cinema of Vengeance*. London: Lorrimer Publishing.

- (1975). 'The Legend of the 7 Golden Vampires', in *Monthly Film Bulletin* v41 n488, pp202-203.

Hearn, M. & Barnes, A. (2007). *The Hammer Story: The Authorised History of Hammer Films*. London: Titan Books.

Hunt, L. (2001). 'Necromancy in the UK: Witchcraft and the Occult in British Horror', in Chibnall, S. & Petley, J. (ed.) *British Horror Cinema*. London & New York: Routledge, pp82-98.

Hunter, I.Q. (2002). 'Hammer Goes East: A Second Glance at *The Legend of the 7 Golden Vampires*, in Mendik, X. (ed.) *Necronomicon Presents: Shocking Cinema of the Seventies*. Hereford: Noir Publishings, pp138-150.

Kei, S. (1994). 'A Brief Historical Tour of the HK Martial Arts Film', in *Bright Lights* n13, pp26-29.

Klemensen, R. (1976). *The House of Hammer Horror*. October, pp16-19.

LaVey, A. S. (1969). *The Satanic Bible*. New York: Avon Books.

Logan, B. (1995). *Hong Kong Action Cinema*. London: Titan Books.

Mayer, G. (2004). *Roy Ward Baker*. Manchester: Manchester University Press.

McGillvray, D. (1974). 'The Legend of the Seven Golden Vampires', in *Cinema TV Today* n10098, p15.

McKay, S. (2007). *A Thing of Unspeakable Horror: The History of Hammer Films*. London: Aurum.

Pirie, D. (2008). *A New Heritage of Horror: The English Gothic Cinema*. London & New York: I.B. Tauris.

Rance, P.T.J. (2005). *Martial Arts Films*. London: Virgin Media Books.

Ransome, N. (2005) 'To the Devil, a screenplay', in *Scriptwriter* n20, pp36-37.

Rigby, J. (2001). 'The Fright of your Life', in *Shivers* n86, p54.

Teo, S. (2005). 'Wuxia Redux: *Crouching Tiger, Hidden Dragon* as a Model of Late Transnational Production', in Meaghan et al. (ed.). *Hong Kong Connections: Transnational Imagination in Action Cinema*. Durham, London & Hong Kong: Duke University Press & Hong Kong University Press, pp191-204.

Time Out. 'The 100 Best Horror Films' www.timeout.com/london/film/the-100-best-horror-films-the-full-list [accessed 10/11/2014].

CHAPTER 8: HAMMER RISES FROM THE GRAVE

In an article in *Empire* magazine, new Hammer CEO Simon Oakes states that *Let Me In* is the first new Hammer release (2010: 39). However, the film, a US-set remake of the Swedish film *Let the Right One In* (2008), was not Hammer's first twenty-first century production. In 2008, the studio released the web series *Beyond the Rave* via MySpace in a conscious attempt to reach the new internet-savvy youth market. The project was somewhat experimental, and released long before online distributors such as Netflix and Amazon began producing material exclusively for their streaming platforms. The production seems to have been airbrushed from history – a search for it on the official Hammer website produces no results. But if it is not exemplary of the relaunched Hammer's output, it begs the question, what does a Hammer film look like in the twenty-first century?

Let Me In

Director Matt Reeves
Year of Release 2010 Running Time 116 minutes Certificate 15

Synopsis: *Los Alamos, New Mexico. A horribly disfigured man, 'Father', is rushed to hospital, where he is visited by Abby, a young girl, and subsequently falls from the tenth floor window to his death. Flashback: Loner Owen is bullied at school and troubled at home. In his mysterious new neighbour Abby, he finds a friendly if diffident companion. Abby, it transpires, is a vampire, forever frozen in time as a teenage girl. 'Father', who lives with Abby, kills a young man in an attempt to drain his blood for her, but fails. Abby eventually has to fend for herself and 'Father' hides the body.*

Meanwhile, Abby and Owen's friendship develops as she convinces him to stand up to the bullies at school. Once more, 'Father' fails in an attempt to source food for Abby, which ultimately leads to his death as seen in the opening sequence. Owen hits bully Kenny on a school trip as the hidden body is found. Afterwards Abby reveals her true self to Owen when he cuts his finger. At the swimming pool, the bullies seek their revenge on Owen, but Abby is waiting for them. The companions leave town together, Abby hidden in a trunk with Owen replacing 'Father' as her protector.

Though director Matt Reeves argues *Let Me In* is not a remake, but rather 'a "weird mélange" of the original film, Lindqvist's novel (and there are aspects of the book in Reeves's film that are absent from Alfreson's), his own experience as a child; and the American setting' (Braund, 2010: 115), one might argue this is exactly what makes it a 'remake'. Such films are rarely exact copies of originals, and even when they attempt to be, as with Gus Van Sant's almost shot-for-shot *Psycho* (1998) experiment, they fail to be exactly the same as their source text. Thomas Leitch suggests that true remakes attempt 'to accommodate the original story to a new discourse' as they 'annihilate the model they are honouring' (2002: 50). In interviews, Reeves often protests that he did not want to destroy the original film, stating, 'I hope [fans] see it and realise how much respect I've paid in maintaining the soul of the original' (in Alexander, 2010: 41). Thus Leitch's definition of the 'true remake' seems somewhat inappropriate to this example. However, the film doesn't comfortably fit within any of the other categories of his taxonomy: it does not make a virtue of greater fidelity to the original literary text than the first film like a 're-adaptation' (though it achieves this slightly, both films excise significant plot points in the novel); it does not attempt purely to 'update' the first film (location aside, there are too many similarities between the films and they were released only two years apart, making an update somewhat pointless); and it is not an 'homage' because it makes significant enough changes in the character names and cultural context to be different enough from the first film.

Michael Druxman uses the term 'direct remake' for films that don't try to hide the fact they are 'based on an earlier production', but may have some changes such as 'a new title [...] updated dialogue, and some "minor" alterations in detail' (1975: 15). Based on the same literary text as *Let the Right One In*, it is no surprise that *Let Me In* is so similar to its cinematic predecessor; there are some sequences which almost seem to be taken shot-for-shot. However, the minor alterations that exist emphasise the American context of the film, typical of so-called 'Hollywood' remakes. It might seem strange to talk of a Hammer film as a Hollywood production, but, as with other recent Hammer films, *Let Me In* is set and filmed in the United States and Exclusive Media, the parent company of Hammer, identifies itself as a global company. Like so many other organisations, Exclusive/Hammer adopts filmmaking traditions usually associated with

'Hollywood' – a term which today has much more fluidity than referring only to the major Los Angeles-based studios. 'Hollywood' films might today be understood as those which retain traditional conventions of narrative storytelling and continuity editing. It is often difficult to distinguish an 'independent' production from one created by the major studios, which have so much control over the industry today and are often involved in so-called 'indie' projects.

As Constantine Verevis contests, much of the literature about remakes 'risk[s] essentialism', adopting a comparative approach which insists that the original is better (2006: 2). This is particularly true when a European film is remade in an American context. There is a long running stigma, which Jennifer Forrest and Leonard R. Koos trace back to the *politiques des auteurs*, that European cinema is superior to American mass culture (2002: 4). Rather than compare the two films in terms of which is the 'best', it is more useful to consider what changes are made in the English language adaptation.

On the face of it, to revisit this particular vampire story so soon after the first film seems strange. Forrest and Koos suggest 'the remake sometimes reflects a director's desire to revisit or rework themes because of what has been called "generic evolution", or because of newly available technology, or because of budgetary restrictions on the original' (2002: 4). One cannot argue that new technology or 'generic evolution' were behind *Let Me In*, released only two years after the original. However 'budgetary restrictions' may be partially relevant. There has been a trend, particularly since the turn of the century, for 'Hollywood' to remake foreign-language genre films, especially horror, exploring what could be done with a bigger budget: other examples include the Spanish film *[REC]* (Dir. Jaumes Balagueró, 2007) transformed into *Quarantine* (John Erick Dowdle, 2008), the J-Horror trend (e.g. *Ringu*, Dir. Hideo Nakata, 1998 / *The Ring*, Dir. Gore Verbinski, 2001) and the Swedish thriller *Girl with the Dragon Tattoo* (*Män som hatar kvinnor*, Dir. Niels Arden Oplev, 2009) remade (Dir. David Fincher, 2011) at a similar time to *Let Me In*. The budget for *Let the Right One In* was approximately $4 million, which became $20 million for the Hammer production. However, crucially, Reeves's film was never intended as a remake, as the script was with Overture Films (Hammer's co-producers) before *Let the Right One In* had been released. The result is an amalgam of original property (the novel) and the Swedish film for an

American audience inflected by director Reeves's own personal approach.

And, indeed, while some have criticised Reeves's film for being almost identical (Debruge, 2010: 42), it is significantly different to *Let the Right One In*. Beyond the Anglicisation of the dialogue and character names, *Let Me In* makes explicit references to American culture in the 1980s both politically, with the inclusion of Reagan's 'Evil Empire' speech, and culturally, with Abby and Owen's trip to the arcade and regular bouts of 80s pop music, including The Vapors and Culture Club. Reeves's film also makes postmodern references to American cinema throughout, assuming the spectator's prior knowledge of classic films which might enable a more complex reading of the narrative. Furthermore, Reeves emphasises the Christian backdrop of the Southern States, but clearly integrates this with the typical Hammer-style Gothic of challenging Manichean distinctions between good and evil. Alongside this adaptation of the content, Reeves adopts conventional 'Hollywood' techniques: a simpler narrative structure (completely removing the subplot of the neighbours that exists in the earlier film); a high impact, suspenseful opening which clearly positions the film as a horror-thriller, setting up vital enigma codes to intrigue the audience; and a diminishing of the complexities of subsidiary characters, such as the young blond bully in the Swedish film, who always seems unwilling to participate in the assaults against Oskar (the Swedish version of Owen).

Let Me In immediately establishes its differences from the original in its opening sequence. While *Let the Right One In* has a linear structure, starting with Oskar stabbing the tree in the courtyard, before the film's main action begins, *Let Me In* starts in the middle of the story, *in media res* (which Bordwell, Staiger and Thompson (1985: 27) contest is typical of Hollywood narrative cinema). White on black text establishes the American context – 'Los Alamos, New Mexico'. These titles instantly tell any spectators familiar with the original that this is an American re-telling of the story. While a similar atmosphere to the original is evoked with the opening dark snowy landscape, the isolation and uncanny calmness is disrupted in the Hammer version with the sound of sirens and the appearance of an ambulance and two police cars. A series of quick cuts proceeds showing a close-up of a radio and shots of a convulsing body in the ambulance. Off-screen we hear, 'male mid-50s with burns over half of his body'. Those who know the first film identify this as a major plot point

– it is the death of the character known only as 'Father'. The sequence culminates in a close-up of Father's injured hand and Abby ending his life at the hospital. As crowds surround his body, which has been dropped from the tenth floor (the seventh in the original film), Reagan's speech plays on a television and the President's face is captured in the reflection of the hospital's windowed-doors. This intense sequence, which positions the spectator in the middle of the action, sets up the typical narrative structure of an American horror-thriller serving as a prologue which establishes the appropriate mood before the linear story unravels. By contrast, *Let the Right One In* takes much more time to introduce the spectator to its horrific moments.

Owen mimics Taxi Driver *in* Let Me In

References to American culture in *Let Me In* persist beyond Reagan's speech. When Owen is introduced he notices a knife in the kitchen and goes to his room. *Let the Right One In* portrays him acting his revenge fantasy first on a tree in the courtyard, and although the same sequence is shown in *Let Me In*, it is pre-empted by a similar scene in his bedroom. Here, Owen wears a mask and turns to his mirror saying 'hey little girl, are you scared' while wielding the knife. He then proceeds to watch his neighbours through a telescope exploring different scenarios: a man lifting weights and a couple engaging in foreplay. This sequence establishes *Let Me In* as an American horror-thriller referencing a number of cinematic predecessors. By adopting the mask in front of the mirror, Owen appropriates the iconography of the typical slasher killer often considered to symbolically lack the phallus – *The Texas Chainsaw Massacre* (Dir. Tobe Hooper, 1974), *Halloween* (Dir. John Carpenter, 1978) and *Friday the 13th* (Dir. Sean S. Cunningham, 1980). By holding the knife and saying 'hey little girl' to his own reflection, he emphasises these American genre conventions. In the Swedish version, he squeals and refers to a pig, which is one of the names he is called by the school bullies, whereas in the re-make, they call him a little girl thus foregrounding questions of gender, which as we will see are actually relevant with regard to Abby's past. Furthermore, Owen mimics Vietnam Vet Travis Bickle (*Taxi Driver*, Dir. Martin Scorsese, 1976) by enacting his fantasy at the mirror. Like Travis, he is the social outsider, who seeks revenge on the people who he feels force him into a life of solitude.

The next sequence in which Owen turns to his telescope is reminiscent of Hitchcock's *Rear Window* (1954), by which Reeves admits he was explicitly influenced. Voyeurism is linked here with scopophilia – the pleasure of looking, in a similar way as it is in Hitchcock's film. Voyeurism is, however, linked to death in *Let Me In*, further emphasising the traditional themes of the American horror film in which frustrations about gender and sexual identity are linked to motivation for murder. It is not only Owen who plays the role of a voyeur in the film, but also 'Father'. Whenever the latter is preparing to kill, deep staging is used to position him as a shadowy figure in the foreground stalking his prey before attacking. *Let Me In* clearly translates the original literary text into the American context, not only through its location and character names, but by adapting sequences so that they conform to conventions typical of Hollywood genre cinema, thus explicating themes of gender and sexuality in different ways to the Swedish film, which shows Eli's (Abby in the US version) lack of genitals (a sequence absent from the US version).

A further technique to Americanise the film is the explication of Christian values. Almost every time Owen's mother is on screen, she says Grace. Towards the end of the film Owen phones his father, asking 'do you think there's such a thing as evil? Can people be evil?' However, his dad dismisses his questions as brainwashing by his mother, whom Owen's dad considers to be obsessed with religion. This sequence is highly significant and absent from the Swedish version. In the first film, even though his parents are separated, Oskar engages in moving scenes with them both – a lyrical synchronised teeth-cleaning moment in which he laughs with his mother, and sledging and playing games with his father, who, it is implied, is an alcoholic. While his parents are divorced, he still enjoys love and affection from them both, even if they are rather distracted. In the American version, their separation deeply affects him – his parents argue on the phone and his father is absent. Abby offers him the companionship he lacks at home, as well as school. The phone sequence particularly emphasises Christian dualism of good/evil, which the Swedish film engages with less explicitly. By removing the neighbour subplot presented in the original film, Reeves encourages an even deeper connection between spectator and Owen (the director explained in interviews that he wanted to tell the story through Owen's eyes because he could relate to the character being bullied and being affected by his own parents' divorce).

Industrially-speaking, Hammer's Americanisation of *Let the Right One In* openly addresses the ambiguity about the 'Britishness' of the studio so revered as part of the nation's cinematic history. As discussed in Chapter Two, Hammer was never wholly British; it always relied on foreign, usually American, funding. But the distinct globalisation of the contemporary film industry further challenges any claim the studio might have to a specific Britishness. As explained, Exclusive is an international business and Hammer's recent output has been set on both sides of the Atlantic, often featuring American stars or intentionally recognised British ones. Consequently, Hammer's new films can be considered 'Hollywood' products in the widest definition of the term.

The Woman in Black

Production Details

Director James Watkins
Year of Release 2012 Running Time 95 minutes Certificate 12A

Synopsis: *Having recently lost his wife, junior solicitor Arthur Kipps is struggling to cope. Encouraged to take an assignment in a distant village, he leaves his young son with his housemaid and travels to Crythin Gifford. Here, he stays in Eel Marsh House in an attempt to review the documents of the recently deceased Alice Drablow. The house is separated from the rest of the village by a frequently flooded causeway and the locals do not seem keen about his visit. Kipps soon discovers that the island and house are haunted by a spectral figure in black, which he eventually realises is the ghost of Alice's sister, Jennet Humfrye. Alice raised Jennet's illegitimate child as her own, but he died in a coach accident on the causeway. Jennet died of ill health some years later, but has haunted the island ever since, and when she appears, a young child in the village always dies.*

As child deaths in the village escalate, Kipps decides to salvage the body of Jennet's son and give him a proper burial. In the meantime, he tries but fails to prevent his own son from coming to visit. As his son and housemaid arrive by train, Kipps believes they are free from the ghost's curse having laid her son to rest, but she appears, as does his dead wife, to take the family to a world beyond this.

While many of Hammer's classic horror films are interested in science, the bourgeois and the possibility of eternal life, the studio's recent productions are often concerned with more immediate domestic issues, such as family and relationship breakdowns and the home as a site of fear. *Wake Wood* focuses on the loss of a child; *The Resident*, a newly-single woman; *Let Me In*, the childlike vampire who seeks a lover/father figure to protect her; and *The Woman in Black* and *Woman in Black Two: Angel of Death* repeat the theme of the lost child. Apart from *The Quiet Ones* and *Beyond the Rave*, all of Hammer's latest productions foreground the domestic space and issues related to it. In contrasting these films with the studio's earlier work, one might suggest there has been a shift from a particularly masculine focus to an emphasis of the female Gothic.

The female Gothic is hardly a new theme for Hammer. Though it is a term most commonly attributed in Film Studies to 1940s Gothic melodramas such as *Gaslight* (Dir. George Cukor, 1944) and *Rebecca* (Dir. Alfred Hitchcock, 1940), Hammer amalgamated these films' prominent themes of the hysterical woman and the instability of the domestic space with the studio's penchant for body horror in its slate of suspense thrillers. The female gothic is particularly evident in *Scream of Fear, Nightmare* (Dir. Freddie Francis, 1964) and *Fear in the Night*, but also persists in some of the period horrors, most notably *The Witches* and *Demons of the Mind* (Dir. Peter Sykes, 1972). And while many of these works play on the theme of the hysterical woman, they often do so only to subvert conventions, for it is often she who is cunning and out-smarts those (usually men) who try to make her suffer. Many of Hammer's hysterical women come to learn that their paranoia was valid, their 'madness' poorly diagnosed and their intelligence and wit sound; they are the films' heroines. Such themes continue in many of the more recent films and *The Woman in Black* offers a particularly interesting engagement with the female Gothic.

The term 'female Gothic' is usually associated with works by women (Wallace & Smith, 2009: 1), thus to apply it to Hammer's films might seem problematic because of the dominance of men at each stage of production (as is regrettably common in the film industry). However, it seems reductive to apply the term only in this way when so many of Hammer's films foreground traditionally feminine concerns. The novel *The Woman in Black* was written by a woman, and Susan Hill, as might be expected from a novel that is a pastiche of the Victorian ghost story, actually exhibits a more traditional image of Victorian masculinity than the film, which makes significant changes to the plot. In Hammer's film, also scripted by a woman (Jane Goldman), Kipps's male body is a site tormented by domestic concerns. He is haunted by the loss of his wife, concerned about the danger that might come to his son and sacrifices himself to be with his family in the afterlife. In the figure of the Woman in Black, he confronts his own fears just as the sequel positions its female protagonist as doppelgänger to the villainess.

While Wallace (2009) reads the metaphor of the woman 'as "dead" or "buried (alive)"' in relation to 'male power structures which render her 'ghostly'' (2009: 26) in pre-twentieth-century texts, the haunting women – Kipps's wife and the Woman in Black – in Hammer's film reflect the fragility of the male as much as they might express a suppression of femininity. One might argue that the Woman in Black's matriarchal control over the children of the village empowers her rather than represents her as a figure of the socially invisible female. The villagers desire not to see her to such an extent that, in the sequel, the remaining survivor makes himself blind. However, she refuses to be invisible. Furthermore, she cannot be defeated by patriarchal society or even another woman who has suffered like her (such as she is matched against in *Angel of Death*). She emanates an eternal power and presence. The spectral here then becomes less about lack of visibility in society and more about omnipotence and omnipresence: ultimate dominance. Wallace notes the Latin root of spectre, 'specere (to look)' (2009:37) and relates it to 'exploring representations of femininity within a symbolic based on visual difference' (ibid.). However, in *The Woman in Black* it is the ghostly titular character who, like the gorgon before her, demands the look from others and is omnipresent, revealing herself in Eve's London home at the end of the sequel.

In Hill's novel, which is told in flashback by Kipps as an aging patriarch, Kipps has a fiancée, Stella, when he leaves for Eel Marsh House and explicitly explains that at that point in his life he had never felt loss. Unlike Hammer's protagonist, he is a confident young man, hoping to better his career. In contrast, Daniel Radcliffe's incarnation is a fragile man, desperate to hold onto his job and consumed by the memory of his dead wife. Radcliffe's Kipps actually finds comfort in the Woman in Black taking the life of him and his son, so he can be reunited with his wife on the other side; while, in the novel, Kipps is devastated when she takes his infant son and wife approximately two years after his visit. The relationship between Kipps and the Woman in Black is represented very differently in the film to the novel. In the film, Kipps's nervousness aligns him with the hysterical gothic woman, but unlike his female counterparts in the films mentioned earlier, he does not successfully vanquish the horror; rather he embraces it, choosing to become ghostly himself. In contrast, in the sequel, Eve is a strong woman who must not only defeat the malign spirit, but nurtures the orphans and her emotionally damaged solider-lover, Harry. Eve believes she has destroyed the Woman in Black, although the audience knows otherwise in the film's closing moments. Regardless, she is a stronger opponent than Kipps.

Locked rooms, like the nursery in *The Woman in Black*, are often associated with the psychoanalytical idea of the primal scene. John Fletcher argues (1995) that the 1940s Gothic melodramas *Rebecca* and *Gaslight* both foreground psychoanalytical primal scenes because

> ...they present an intrusion into a space which has been the scene of a desiring and/or murderous action in the past. This scene is speculated upon, imagined, remembered; it is not represented by the film directly but is present in its traces, which are encrypted or embalmed in a sealed, preserved room. (1995: 344)

The Woman in Black continues this convention of Gothic melodrama revealing the malleability of the 'Gothic' label as a term which transcends traditional genre distinctions as the locked nursery becomes a site of horror. Psychoanalytical theory has often been criticised for being male-centric, as discussed in earlier chapters, therefore it might seem strange to consider the primal scene as relevant to the female Gothic. However, Fletcher, influenced by Raymond Durgnat's observations, considers these female Gothic films to exhibit a feminine Oedipal trajectory: the heroine marries the father figure after facing an older rival from his past (1995: 346). While *The Woman in Black* contains the mysterious locked room, the film's spectre does not follow the Oedipus narrative. The Woman in Black takes refuge in the house, she is not trapped there by others, and entices Kipps and later Eve to come into the forbidden room. The Woman in Black continually seeks to return to her primal scene rather than repress it, and it becomes a site of mourning and memory, for she continually cries out 'never forget'.

Kipps takes the position of The Woman in Black, in so doing acknowledging his own traumatic state

When Kipps enters the nursery, he takes the position of the Woman in Black mirroring her body language and gazing through the window at the spot where he had been standing when she looked down upon him on his arrival at the house. In taking her position he becomes her doppelgänger and reveals a shared desire to remain with the past. While she takes children to replace her own, he sacrifices himself and his son to return to his dead wife. His commitment to finding the corpse of her son emphasises his belief that they have shared desires. However, there is one stark contrast between the two. While Kipps is content to return to the past, the Woman in Black is not, and continues to kill children, acting out her trauma repeatedly.

Trauma theorist Cathy Caruth defines two significant features of trauma which are illustrated in *The Woman in Black*. She explains that mental trauma is 'an event that [...] is experienced too soon, too unexpectedly, to be fully known and is therefore not available to consciousness until it imposes itself again, repeatedly in the nightmares and repetitive actions of the survivor' (Caruth, 1996: 4); as such it is a double wound always characterised by repetition. Secondly, reading Freud's interpretation of the romantic epic *Gerusalemme Liberata*, she suggests trauma is also informed by a voice which 'bears witness to the past' that has been 'unwittingly repeated' (Caruth, 1996: 3). Considering these two characteristics, *The Woman in Black* can be understood as a traumatic narrative. The carriage accident – the original traumatic act – is repeated throughout the film: first as a ghostly sound, then as an apparition, and finally as a real event as Kipps risks his own life in attempt to salvage the boy's body. Furthermore, Kipps is called to bear witness to the past through the spectres that haunt him. While the Woman in Black seeks him to take her position as witness to the death of her son, his wife too appears as a voice, in the opening scene and later as 'the Woman in White'. It is the repeated presence of these women that keeps him locked in a traumatic episode, his mental incarceration visualised by the isolation of Eel Marsh House.

Trauma, melancholy, loss and mourning foreground liminality and ambiguity, blurring comprehension about spatial and temporal boundaries. In this respect, they are perfect subjects for the Gothic, and for Hammer. Both *Woman in Black* films foreground feminine trauma, but present their female ghostly body as a relentlessly revengeful being that shows neither remorse nor desire to heal. In contrast, their male characters are fragile and desire reconciliation with the past, and thus they offer interesting contemporary revisions of traditional female Gothic types. In these films, it is the male body that is a site for hysteria, worked through and resolved (by death or with the help of a female counterpart); the female body continually calls to be looked at and then, like the gorgon's stare, inflicts pain on those who turn their gaze towards it.

References

Alexander, C. (2010). 'Hammer Horror: *Let Me In*: The Vampire Transplant', in *Fangoria* n297, p39-41.

Bordwell, D et al. (1985) 'Classical narration', in *The Classical Hollywood Cinema, Film Style and the Mode of Production to 1960*. London: Routledge.

Braund, S. (2010). 'The Outsiders', in *Empire* n257, p116-118, 121.

Caruth, C. (1996). *Unclaimed Experience: Trauma, Narrative and History*. Baltimore & London: The Johns Hopkins University Press.

Debruge, P. (2010). 'Let Me In' review, in *Variety* 20th September, p42.

Druxman, M. B. (1975). *Make It Again Sam, A Survey of Movie Remakes*. South Brunswick & New York, and London: A.S. Barnes and Company and Thomas Yoseloff Ltd.

Fletcher, J. (1995). 'Primal Scenes and the Female Gothic: *Rebecca* and *Gaslight*', in *Screen* v36 n4, pp 341-370.

Forrest, J. and Koos, L.R. (ed.). (2002). *Dead Ringers: The Remake in Theory and Practice*. Albany: State University of New York Press.

Hill, S. (2012). *The Woman in Black*. London: Vintage.

Leitch, T. (2002). 'Twice-Told Tales: Disavowal and the Rhetoric of the Remake', in Forrest, J. and Koos, L. R. (ed.). *Dead Ringers: The Remake in Theory and Practice*. Albany: State University of New York Press, pp37-62.

Verevis, C. (2006). *Film Remakes*. Edinburgh: Edinburgh University Press.

Wallace, D. (2009). ''The Haunting Idea': Female Gothic Metaphors and Feminist Theory', in Wallace, D. & Smith, A. (ed.). *The Female Gothic New Directions*. Basingstoke: Palgrave Macmillan, pp26-41.

Wallace, D. & Smith, A. (2009). 'Introduction: Defining the Female Gothic', in Wallace, D. & Smith, A. (ed.). *The Female Gothic New Directions*. Basingstoke: Palgrave Macmillan, pp1-13.

CONCLUSION

Hammer has long been celebrated as the most significant horror producer in the history of British cinema, however as we have seen, the national identity of these films has always been fluid because of the studio's reliance on overseas financing, and the studio is now part of a global organisation. Despite the international conditions of the films' productions, they have nonetheless often, apart from perhaps some of the more recent films, grappled with specifically British themes or a particular Gothic style which deeply resonates with British people and invokes a specific type of Britishness for foreign audiences. Terence Fisher's films, particularly, embody a restraint and an ambiguous representation of genders, classes and regions, often on the surface seeming to evidence clear binary opposites but when the films are investigated more deeply, things are not so black and white. These two levels of inference emphasise the notion of 'keeping up appearances' so embedded in British culture historically and the ambiguity of British identity at the time (1950s–1970s), when great social upheavals were underway.

While the great 'family' studio of the past has gone, Hammer CEO Simon Oakes states that he and his team 'have a family growing here, that's just starting' (Alexander, 2010: 41), and there are clearly thematic repetitions across the twenty-first century oeuvre. However, while the old films stuck to very particular conventions, eventually to the point of unoriginality for the sake of profit, Oakes's team have produced a series of individually distinct films, aside from their generic similarity. These new Hammer horrors may not yet have attained the same cult status, and they are clearly products of the contemporary globalised industry, but this certainly does not make them lesser films, and in *The Woman in Black* the company scored a bona fide international hit. With much larger budgets, Hammer is now able to indulge in more sophisticated projects.

Hammer is a true icon of cinema, not only in Britain, but internationally. The original films are still popular today, and examples of cinema's juxtaposition of storytelling and attraction, often repeating classic tales while offering spaces to experience spectacle, shocks and titillation. The first British colour horror films remain wonders of the archives and have influenced a wide range of filmmakers in the UK and abroad. These Gothic gems may have been considered 'trash cinema' at the time, but they are sophisticated works which have the potential to engage spectators with a wide range of issues. Furthermore the Gothic themes resonate beyond the classic colour films and reverberate through Hammer's thrillers such as *Scream of Fear* and even some of their so-called adventure films, such as *The Stranglers of Bombay*. However, despite the box office achievements of its prehistoric adventures and the studio's foray into science fiction, thrillers and even comedies (we must not forget *On the Buses* (Dir. Harry Booth, 1971)), it is its horror films which have fuelled its lasting success. This was clearly noted by Oakes and his team, who have revived the Hammer horror legacy in the twenty-first century.

Yet, as in the past, today's industry is not simple. Since this book was first contracted, Exclusive's library and rights to several sequels and development projects have been sold to AMBI Group. Hammer's website has not announced a new film production since the *Woman in Black* sequel. However the company now has a thriving fiction imprint, has announced a partnership with Titan Comics and is co-producer of a play of Shirley Jackson's terrifying novel, *The Haunting of Hill House*, which premiered in Liverpool in 2015. Hammer in the twenty-first century is a multimedia organisation.

FILMOGRAPHY

Hammer films mentioned in this book

The Abominable Snowman (Dir. Terence Fisher, 1957)

The Anniversary (Dir. Roy Ward Baker, 1968)

Beyond the Rave (Dir. Matthias Hoene, 2008)

Brides of Dracula (Dir. Terence Fisher, 1960)

The Camp on Blood Island (Dir. Val Guest, 1958)

Captain Clegg (Dir. Peter Graham Scott, 1962)

Captain Kronos, Vampire Hunter (Dir. Brian Clemens, 1974)

Countess Dracula (Dir. Peter Sasdy, 1971)

The Curse of Frankenstein (Dir. Terence Fisher, 1957)

The Curse of the Werewolf (Dir. Terence Fisher, 1961)

Demons of the Mind (Dir. Peter Sykes, 1972)

The Devil Rides Out (Dir. Terence Fisher, 1968)

Dr. Jekyll and Sister Hyde (Dir. Seth Holt, 1971)

Dracula (Dir. Terence Fisher, 1958)

Dracula A.D 1972 (Dir. Alan Gibson, 1972)

Dracula has Risen from the Grave (Dir. Freddie Francis, 1968)

Dracula, Prince of Darkness (Dir. Terence Fisher, 1966)

Fear in the Night (Dir. Jimmy Sangster, 1972)

Four-Sided Triangle (Dir. Terence Fisher, 1953)

Frankenstein Created Woman (Dir. Terence Fisher, 1967)

Frankenstein Must Be Destroyed (Dir. Terence Fisher, 1969)

The Gorgon (Dir. John Gilling, 1964)

The Hound of the Baskervilles (Dir. Terence Fisher, 1959)

Horror of Frankenstein (Dir. Jimmy Sangster, 1970)

Kiss of the Vampire (Dir. Don Sharp, 1963)

The Lady Vanishes (Dir. Anthony Page, 1979)

The Legend of the 7 Golden Vampires (Dir. Roy Ward Baker, 1974)

Let Me In (Dir. Matt Reeves, 2010)

The Lost Continent (Dir. Michael Carreras, 1968)

The Man in Black (Dir. Francis Searle, 1949)

The Man Who Could Cheat Death (Dir. Terence Fisher, 1959)

The Mummy (Dir. Terence Fisher, 1959)

Never Take Sweets from a Stranger (Dir. Cyril Frankel, 1960)

Nightmare (Dir. Freddie Francis, 1964)

The Old Dark House (Dir. William Castle, 1963)

On the Buses (Dir. Harry Booth, 1971)

The Quatermass Xperiment (Dir. Val Guest, 1955)

Quatermass II (Dir. Val Guest, 1957)

Quatermass and the Pit (Dir. Roy Ward Baker, 1968)

The Quiet Ones (Dir. John Pogue, 2014)

The Phantom of the Opera (Dir. Terence Fisher, 1962)

The Plague of Zombies (Dir. John Gilling, 1966)

Rasputin the Mad Monk (Dir. Don Sharp, 1966)

The Reptile (Dir. John Gilling, 1966)

The Resident (Dir. Antti Jokinen, 2011)

Scars of Dracula (Dir. Roy Ward Baker, 1970)

Scream of Fear (Dir. Seth Holt, 1961)

Seven Brothers Meet Dracula (Dir. Roy Ward Baker, 1974)

Shatter (Dir. Michael Carreras, 1974)

The Snorkel (Dir. Guy Green, 1958)

The Stranglers of Bombay (Dir. Terence Fisher, 1959)

To the Devil a Daughter (Dir. Peter Sykes, 1976)

Twins of Evil (Dir. John Hough, 1971)

The Two Faces of Dr Jekyll (Dir. Terence Fisher, 1960)

Ugly Duckling (Dir. Lance Comfort, 1959)

Vampire Lovers (Dir. Roy Ward Baker, 1970)

Wake Wood (Dir. David Keating, 2010)

The Witches (Dir. Cyril Frankel, 1966)

The Women in Black (Dir. James Watkins, 2012)

The Woman in Black 2: Angel of Death (Dir. Tom Harper, 2014)

X the Unknown (Dir. Joseph Losey, 1956)

Television and Documentary

Greasepaint and Gore (Dir. Russell Wall, 2004)

Hammer House of Horror (1980)

Hammer House of Mystery and Suspense (1984)

Other films mentioned

The Astonished Heart (Dir. Anthony Darnborough & Terence Fisher, 1950)

The Blair Witch Project (Dir. Daniel Myrick & Eduardo Sánchez, 1999)

Bonnie and Clyde (Dir. Arthur Penn, 1967)

A Chinese Ghost Story (Dir. Siu-Tung Ching, 1987)

A Clockwork Orange (Dir. Stanley Kubrick, 1971)

Cloverfield (Dir. Matt Reeves, 2008)

Colonel Bogey (Dir. Terence Fisher, 1948)

Count Yorga, Vampire (Dir. Ben Kelljan, 1970)

Dakula halála (*The Death of Drakula*, Károly Lajthay, 1921)

The Devils (Dir. Ken Russell, 1971)

Encounters of a Spooky Kind (Dir. Sammo Kam-Bo Hung, 1980)

Evil Dead: Army of Darkness (Dir. Sam Raimi, 1992)

Frankenstein (Dir. James Whale, 1931)

Frankenstein's Monster (Dir. J. Searle Dawley, 1910)

Friday the 13th (Dir. Sean S. Cunningham, 1980)

Gaslight (Dir. George Cukor, 1944)

Girl with the Dragon Tattoo (*Män som hatar kvinnor*, Dir. Niels Arden Oplev, 2009)

Girl with the Dragon Tattoo (Dir. David Fincher, 2011)

Halloween (Dir. John Carpenter, 1978)

I Spit on Your Grave (Dir. Meir Zarchi, 1978)

Last House on the Left (Dir. Wes Craven, 1972)

Let the Right One In (Dir. Tomas Alfredson, 2008)

The Lord of the Rings (Dir. Peter Jackson, 2001-2003)

Le manoir du diable (Dir. Georges Méliès, 1986)

Martin (Dir. George A. Romero, 1976)

Mr Vampire (Dir. Ricky Lau, 1985)

Night of the Living Dead (Dir. George A. Romero, 1968)

Nosferatu (Dir. R.W. Murnau, 1922)

Peeping Tom (Dir. Michael Powell, 1960)

Photographing a Ghost (Dir. George Albert Smith, 1987)

Psycho (Dir. Alfred Hitchcock, 1960)

Psycho (Dir. Gus Van Sant, 1998)

The Quatermass Experiment [TV] (1953)

Quarantine (Dir. John Erick Dowdle, 2008)

Rear Window (Dir. Alfred Hitchcock, 1954)

Rebecca (Dir. Alfred Hitchcock, 1940)

[REC] (Dir. James Balagueró, 2007)

Repulsion (Dir. Roman Polanski, 1965)

The Ring (Dir. Gore Verbinski, 2002)

Ringu (Dir. Hideo Nakata, 1998)

The Rocky Horror Picture Show (Dir. Jim Sharman, 1975)

Rosemary's Baby (Dir. Roman Polanski, 1968)

Star Wars (Dir. George Lucas, 1977)

Taxi Driver (Dir. Martin Scorsese, 1976)

The Texas Chainsaw Massacre (Dir. Tobe Hooper, 1974)

We are Going to Eat You (Dir. Hark Tsui, 1980)

The Wild Bunch (Dir. Sam Peckinpah, 1969)

Witchfinder General (Dir. Michael Reeves, 1968),

The Wicker Man (Dir. Robin Hardy, 1973)

Frightmares
A History of British Horror Cinema
Ian Cooper

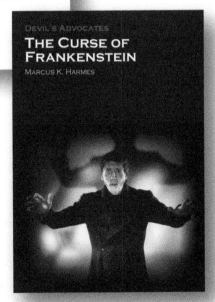

DEVIL'S ADVOCATES
THE CURSE OF
FRANKENSTEIN
MARCUS K. HARMES